To Barbara ☐
I am so pleased I
have gotten to know you
in this wonderful
community.
Kindly
Lois

The Last Chapter

LOIS B. GREEN

WITH LAURA SMITH PORTER

the **Peppertree Press**
Sarasota, Florida

ISBN: 978-1-936051-72-4
Library of Congress Number: 2009941098

Printed in the U.S.A.
Printed November 2009

TO BOB,

who gave me the love, wise counsel and freedom
to discover the woman I wanted to become.

Acknowledgements

My heartfelt thanks to the following people who had a part in the making of this book:

First and foremost, Laura Porter, who was recommended to me by a mutual friend and became my alter ego as we wrote this book together over the last sixteen months. Laura is a freelance writer and editor whose work has appeared in newspapers, magazines and anthologies including a weekly column, "Dispatches from the Home Front" for the *Worcester Telegram and Gazette*. She has a Ph.D. in American History from Princeton University and lives nearby in Worcester.

Ken David, who, when he heard that I read the last chapter of every book first, quickly recognized the perfect title for this book;

Joan Gage, who graciously reviewed the book and made many useful comments;

Elizabeth Cooney, who read the final manuscript and made suggestions to improve its clarity;

Julie Ann Howell, whom I immediately picked as my publisher when I saw the owl on her desk and learned her pre-school students called her "Mrs. Owl."

And to the following for making my chapters happy ones:

Kathy Edmiston, my oncologist, who has treated me for my cancer and sustained my spirit over the past nine years;

Peter Levine, who has helped me through every crisis and always given me hope;

Barbara Greenberg and Joan Sadowsky, who have been my closest friends for over fifty-seven years;

My sister, Jean Helliesen, and all my cousins, who were part of my extended family and remain close until this day;

Lenny and Norman Asher, who have been by my side since Norman introduced Bob to me sixty years ago;

If it were possible, I would name every person who cared for and supported me throughout my life. Certainly, my grandmother, my Aunt Fran, Annie and my brother, Joel, gave me the loving foundation I needed to make it through a difficult childhood.

My children, in-law children and grandchildren, whose unconditional love surrounds me;

And finally, to all of my friends, too many to name, from The Seasons, Sarasota and Worcester, who have given me laughter, kindness and the joy of living every day to its fullest.

I treasure each of you.

THE LAST CHAPTER

OLD LADY'S PRAYER

"Lord, thou knowest that I am growing older.
Keep me from becoming talkative and possessed with
the idea that I must express myself on every subject.
Release me from the craving to straighten out
everyone's affairs. Keep my mind free
from the recital of endless detail.

Give me wings to get to the point. Seal my lips
when I am inclined to tell of my aches and pains.
They are increasing with the years and my love
to speak of them grows sweeter as time goes by.

Teach me the glorious lesson that occasionally
I may be wrong. Make me thoughtful but not nosy –
helpful but not bossy.

With my vast store of wisdom and experience,
it does seem a pity not to use it all. But thou knowest, Lord,
that I want a few friends at the end."

-Anonymous

PROLOGUE

"What do you know now that you wish you had known at 30?" That was a question asked of me recently when I was videotaped as part of a presentation for an awards ceremony for young leaders. I mulled over the question for a bit before the answer came to me. What do I wish I had known almost fifty years ago? I wish I had known how brief life was and how quickly it would speed by. How much time we all spend planning ahead, forgetting to enjoy the here and the now!

In 2001, I was diagnosed with breast cancer, which necessitated a lumpectomy followed by chemotherapy and radiation. Four years later, a second diagnosis confirmed another primary site cancer in the other breast, requiring the same scenario as the first. Two years after that, in August 2007, I was told that it had metastasized to both lungs. At the same time, I was also informed I was triple negative, meaning I did not have any of the positive receptors that might have afforded more treatments and lengthened my poor prognosis. That was not to be in the cards that God had dealt me.

Amazingly, the prospect of death, coward though I am, has not been as frightening as I had expected. Since I was a child, I have always read the last chapter of every book first. And so it is inevitable that I think a lot about my own last chapter, wondering about the prospect of dying and what the end might be like. I imagine that I am in my home, surrounded by those I love the most: my children, my in-law children, and my grandchildren. Perhaps I have even had my friends over during the week to share a last goodbye and drink a glass of wine. If I am really fortunate, the cancer will not have reached areas that might spoil the ending I have imagined. That last chapter has not been written, so I can't read it ahead of time. Perhaps I should be glad.

It is difficult to explain, but these past months since August 2007 have been some of the happiest of my entire life. I consider it a gift from God that knowing my prognosis has allowed me to enjoy life as I never have before.

I have done everything I want to do and all the things that bring me joy. The best is our Thanksgiving family reunion in Longboat Key, Florida, where eighteen of us come together from all over the country to hug, laugh, tell stories, play games and enjoy every minute of every day. We all know it may be our last Thanksgiving together, but that doesn't spoil it; it only makes it more special. We have created a tradition that no one will ever forget, a legacy that Pop-pop, my late husband, Bob, began twelve years ago and has become the highlight of each year for all of us. My daughter-in-law, Wendy Zevin, has captured the moments of our family in photograph after photograph, images that will survive us all.

And what joy I have seeing my old friends and making new ones. In 2002, after Bob died, I moved into the Seasons, a retirement community in Holden, only four miles from our home of 48 years in Worcester. I often say that God wanted to make up to me for all my problems, so he dropped me into the Seasons, where I have made many new, loving and caring friends. I also spend the winter in Florida and participate in community activities both in Longboat Key and Sarasota. In addition to my old friends, I have a wide circle of new friends who share my interests. I feel so privileged. So many people don't understand that opening up to the possibility of new friendships adds a broader, richer dimension to one's life. A friend of mine always asks me, "And how many new friends did you make today?" I love to tell the story of how I once met someone in the security line at the airport. She insisted she knew me. She knew that my name was Lois, that I lived in Worcester, and that my husband was in the insurance business but until this day has no idea how she knew all those things. She promptly invited me to her New Year's Day party. Edie Chaifetz and I have since become friends.

How many people think they will live forever and don't stop to enjoy the moment! Have they ever looked at the brilliant colors of the changing leaves, enjoyed the sunset on the water or listened to a beautiful concert, knowing they might soon not have that pleasure?

How many talk to their children and grandchildren consciously realizing they might not have many more chances to do so?

And how many use their voices to speak up to right wrongs, appreciating that life will soon end and there is no time to wait?

Knowing I don't have much time left also forces me to review my life. In these pages, I contemplate all of the wonderful things that have happened to me over the years and the accomplishments that have made me so proud. From the Worcester Jewish Federation to the United Way, from Elder Home Care to Memorial Hospital, all in Worcester, and nationally from the Council of Jewish Federations to the United Jewish Appeal to the American Hospital Association, I have worked hard to become a force for change, asking difficult questions and seeking allies to improve our community in a myriad of ways. No matter what I have done, I have been able to rely on my husband Bob's constancy and the love of my family and friends, who have always come first.

On the other hand, I also recall the painful parts of my life, hoping the passage of time might have dulled some of that ache. Yet my eyes still fill up when I recall aspects of my childhood. Raised in a house of formidable women, I feared my mother's disapproval even as I loved her. I was haunted by her cruelties to me. My grandmother taught me the importance of a life lived philanthropically but suffered from a mental illness that at times permeated our household. I was terrified of my stepfather's quick temper, often unleashed at me. But I had my brother, Joel, my grandmother's housekeeper, Annie, my Aunt Fran and adored baby cousin, Judy, and – always -summers at the beach.

I learned to cope early, turning over in my bed at night and listening to the Brooklyn Dodgers games on my radio so I could not hear my mother's arguing with my stepfather about me. When I was old enough, I escaped to boarding school.

Sometimes I believe that the little girl looking for love still cries inside me. Is it possible I might even be grateful that surviving those early years has made me the woman I am today? Now that the end is in sight, I wonder.

And perhaps that is the real last chapter.

CHAPTER ONE

GROWING UP IN WEST HARTFORD

*"Today's responsible parents strive to raise children with
healthy egos. But for a lot of adults, the word 'ego' carries the
negative connotation of 'narcissism.' Traditionally, the 'good'
child learned self-control, self-denial and placed parental needs
and wishes first. If those needs were abusive to the child, there
was no choice but to block the hurtful behavior in order to hold
onto adults who were loved and needed."*

- Alice Miller, Prisoners of Childhood

My earliest memory of West Hartford was of a funky little
yellow house on Stratford Road, where my mother, my
sister, Jean, my brother, Joel, and I lived with my grandmother
and my Aunt Fran, whom my grandmother had brought home to
care for after Fran's mother died. We had a very close extended
family. My mother's brother and his wife, Sam and Helen, and

their two children, Rachel and Nancy, lived next door to my grandmother. Her sister -- my Aunt Min -- and her husband, Uncle John, lived with their three children, Michael, Danny and Peter, high on a hill above and behind us. Still another uncle and aunt, Eddie and Eddy, lived less than half a mile away with their family, Michael, Richard and later Johnny.

My parents, Adeline Suisman and Herman (Hermie) Goldstein, had divorced in 1932, when I was two years old. They had separated earlier but then tried once more to make their marriage work. I was the result of that attempt – a "reconciliation baby," my sister says -- though their reconciliation didn't last very long. Indeed, twenty minutes after I was born, I was covered head to toe with eczema, which must have come from the enormous stress my mother was under regarding her marriage.

After a short time at my grandmother's house on Stratford Road, my mother took all of us back to the nearby home she and my father had built together and where we had lived when I was first born. My grandmother, Fran and my grandmother's maid, Annie, all came with us. It was in this beautiful brick house on Foxcroft Road that I grew up. During a childhood that was often painful, my close relationship with my brother, Joel, only sixteen months older, sustained me. So, too, did my grandmother's love, as well the warm and reassuring presence of Annie, to whom I ran when I needed comfort, and Fran, whom I adored.

My mother, by contrast, offered only inconsistent affection. I think now that she probably never wanted me. When I was very little, only three or four years old, she delighted – and I can only say delighted – in telling me that she had found me abandoned on the doorstep because nobody had wanted me. When I cried, devastated by the story, she would put me in her lap and tell me it wasn't true. I can still see the chair where we sat together, a green club chair in front of the fireplace in the living room on Foxcroft Road. I have a family photograph taken there, my mother sitting in the chair with the three of us grouped around her. "You told me it wasn't true!" I would cry the next time she told me the awful story. "Oh, no," she would say. "It was true." And the pattern repeated itself.

Looking back, I recognize that she was a single parent with no money of her own, raising three children at the height of the Depression. My uncles used to come and leave money for her on top of the piano. We were very poor, though I didn't realize it at the time because we lived with my wealthy grandmother. She employed not only Annie, but also a chauffeur, named Mike, and she used her considerable resources to pay for everything. Until my mother remarried when I was eight years old and my stepfather, Harry, began to support us, she was totally dependent on my grandmother. It must have been quite difficult for her in those years.

When we were very small, she regularly put my brother and me to bed very early, around six o'clock in the evening, so early that it was still light out, and we could hear the other children playing out on the street. No doubt sending us to sleep right after dinner was a way for her to reclaim some time for herself. Yet it was a lonely feeling to lie in bed, listening to the shrieks and laughter of the neighborhood children.

I loved my mother, but I was also afraid of her and wary of her unpredictability. That was the dynamic that drove our relationship. She was incredibly strict, never reneging on either a punishment or a promise. When I had children myself, she would read them *Horton Hears a Who!* by Dr. Seuss. "I meant what I said and I said what I meant," she would recite. "An elephant's faithful, 100 percent." The line never failed to remind me of my own childhood.

For my mother, punishment often meant taking us into the room over the garage, where we stored big boxes. Joel and I played hide-and-seek there, but when we were in trouble, my mother grabbed us by the hand, took us into the playroom and hit us on the backside with a belt. Joel was anxious to please and tried hard to behave. I did, too (I don't ever remember talking back to her), but I was often punished for being outspoken. One day, we got on the bus to go downtown and the bus driver asked "Is she under six?" (Children who were under six rode free.) When my mother told him I was only five, I retorted, "Mom, you're a liar. That's not true!" I had been taught that lying was wrong. I got in trouble for that.

Another time, I was sent to my room for some transgression or another. When I heard that everyone else in the family was going to the movies, I came downstairs and apologized to my mother. "I won't do that anymore," I told her. "I'm really glad," she said. "Now go back upstairs to your room." They all went to the movies without me. That was the kind of discipline that she thought was important. Was it? I don't know now whether she was right or wrong, but she certainly didn't give me a lot of reasons to believe that she liked me. To this day, I really don't know.

Though I felt singled out by her disapproval, my brother and sister were equally convinced that our mother was partial to me. I had terrible table manners, but Mother never corrected me. Jean, four years older than I, remembers picketing in front of our house with Joel, both of them wearing placards to protest my preferential treatment. At the same time, my sister believes that our mother never really liked having any of us. Indeed, she was a Dr. Jekyll and Mr. Hyde, taking us to the movies one moment and turning on us the next. She could be cute and funny, but she saved much of that behavior for her nieces and nephews and her grandchildren, all of whom thought she was wonderful. She was known for being a loving and generous friend, dropping everything to run to someone in trouble. I'm always struck by stories of her kindness to others; it seems as though the outside world saw a completely different person.

Jean talked back to Mother. In fact, Mother was a little afraid of Jean because she stood up for herself. When my mother and grandmother spoke in Yiddish at the dinner table so that we couldn't understand them, Jean learned the language and told Joel and me everything they said. Her own resentment of Mother ran deep, in part because when she later married a Norwegian doctor, a non-Jew, Mother gave him the cold shoulder and would not support Jean in her senior year at college. When Mother died, years later, Jean refused to wear a black ribbon or sit in the room reserved for family.

For all of us, Fran Shapiro helped lighten the atmosphere in the house. Fran was young when she came to live with our grandmother and already sixteen when I was born. She was part of my life the whole time I was growing up, an adored aunt and constant source of affection. She was very pretty, and when she dated, she and her current boyfriend would often take Joel and me out for ice cream. Once she had a boyfriend who had a little car with a rumble seat in the back. Joel and I used to sit in the rumble seat and pray that she would marry him. But, instead, she married Sid Kaplan and moved into Hartford, to a little brick apartment building on Huntington Avenue. Here they had my cousin, Judy. The most wonderful thing that ever happened to me was the birth of Judy. I was eleven years old, I was sick in bed, and I made a baby book for Judy when she was born. The happiest days were when I went over to visit Judy in that apartment. Fran, Sid, Judy, and Debby, their younger daughter, also stayed with us at the beach in the summers, which is why I have remained close to those cousins my whole life.

My brother, Joel, and I were sixteen months apart and inseparable. He used to walk me to elementary school, a small neighborhood school called Beach Park School that our cousins also attended. There was a policeman at the corner named Bill, whom we loved; he had a little dog and used to help us cross the street. Beach Park had a fishpond in the kindergarten, and there was only one grade per class. I remember the name of almost every teacher I had at Beach Park. I loved most of them; they were wonderful to me because I always got very good grades. (None of us liked Miss Ring, our fifth grade teacher, who was very strict.) Miss Black, the art teacher who came to give us lessons, used to say to me, "'Loyse,' you're not trying!" Of course, I had absolutely no talent whatsoever. I still have a little charcoal sketch that I did for her, framed and hanging on my upstairs hall. My children laugh at me whenever I ask which of them would like it.

I do remember being self-conscious about being Jewish when I was in elementary school. It was the only time I ever felt different. In my class, there was only one other Jewish child besides me, Ernest Goldberg, who lived two doors away from us on Foxcroft Road. There were loads of Jewish kids in my brother's class, but not in mine. So when we received a small gift for Hanukkah, a book or some Hanukkah gelt, I would go to school and make up a list of toys that Santa Claus had brought me for Christmas. I no longer remember whether I didn't want to be different, or I didn't want them to know I was Jewish. They must have known, though, because we were always out of school for the Jewish holidays.

We belonged to the Emanuel Synagogue on Woodland Street in Hartford, then the largest Conservative synagogue in Connecticut. At the time, Jews were in the process of moving west from the city, but the institutions remained in Hartford. I had Sunday school friends from Hartford and other friends in my neighborhood in West Hartford. (To this day I never say that I come from "West Hartford," which would have been considered snobby. Whenever I refer to Hartford, it really means West Hartford.) Ernest Goldberg and I were friends. When we were in the fifth grade, he was the one who told me where babies came from. (I told him he was a big liar and that babies actually came from the belly button.)

But my brother was my best friend. We used to tie string to tin cans and use them to talk back and forth from his room to mine. At that time, kids traded playing cards, buying decks and collecting pairs of cards. Sometimes, at school, we would throw the decks on the ground in a scramble, and Joel would dive in to get cards for me. When my room was messy, he would come in and clean it up so I wouldn't get yelled at. He was sensitive; he wanted peace in the family. When we played house, he pretended that he was the father who was going off to work and then left me to play alone. He was too kind to tell me he didn't want to play, and I never caught on.

My mother was rarely home. She was often off playing cards or involved in activities with the synagogue sisterhood. From the time I was little, my grandmother's maid, Annie, took care of me. She was a small Polish woman who wore her gray hair in a bun and whose English was slightly stilted. The melody of her language was a constant in my life. For example, she would tell my grandmother we needed some more "towel papers." I loved Annie. It was she who combed my long brown hair into braids every morning and saved the frosting for me when she made a cake. She was there when I came home for lunch and from school every afternoon. She gave me my milk and cookies, and it was to her I ran whenever I was hurt or afraid.

When I was very small, my bedroom was directly above the sun parlor; one had to go through my mother's room to reach it. I was terrified to go to sleep. The branch of the huge maple just outside brushed against the window, and I was convinced that someone would climb the tree, come in the window and steal me away. I don't remember any conversations about the kidnapping of the Lindbergh baby when I was a child, though it is likely that the details of the 1932 crime would have been commonly discussed. But I do remember my fear. I was certain that nobody would be able to hear my screams and save me; my room was off on the side of the house and too far away from the rest of the family in the evenings. Only Annie knew how scared I was. Every night, she turned on a light in my mother's room, sat down in a chair and opened my door. I could peek through the crack and see her. She never told anybody, because she knew that my mother would say that I needed to get over my fear. And so she sat there every night with me until I rolled over and went to sleep.

Our house was the center of our large extended family because of my grandmother, a true matriarch whose genes, for better or worse, I believe I have inherited. Sarah P. Suisman was an independent, determined, strong, bossy and controlling woman, whose example showed me the importance of self-confidence. She was very kind to me, leaving no doubt in my mind that she loved me very much. She took us on trips to Miami Beach, Atlantic City in New Jersey and Sharon Springs in New York. Moreover, she set the tone for community responsibility that defined all of us.

We were an active family, prominent in the Jewish community. My grandmother was one of the founders of the Hebrew Home for the Aged and involved in many philanthropic efforts. My mother started the Women's Division of the Jewish Federation. My uncles, her brothers Edward and Samuel, ran a scrap metal business, Suisman & Blumenthal, which their father had begun in 1899. Samuel Suisman started Mount Sinai Hospital, and Edward was a founder of the Jewish Federation of Hartford as well as its first president. They were all incredibly generous givers. During the Second World War, my uncles founded the Suisman Foundation, which helped to support schools, hospitals and social agencies. They were also involved with helping Israel, before and after the state was founded.

I literally learned about the importance of philanthropy at my grandmother's side. One stormy September day in 1938, she took me with her to the Hebrew Home for the Aged to inspect the new plumbing that had been installed that day. She was a very active member of the Board of Directors, probably the chairman. Torrential rain was falling, and the wind howled: we were in the middle of the hurricane of 1938. But my grandmother felt responsible for the wellbeing of the residents. Nothing would have deterred her from doing what she thought needed to be done, even if we were in danger.

She often let me ride along with her and her chauffeur, Mike, when she collected for raffles and other causes from her women friends. (Mike sometimes drove Joel and me to school.) I went up to the door with her when she went from house to house, visiting Mrs. Lashiver or Mrs. Weiner. She taught me how to make hospital corners, standing over me to make sure that each side was equal when I made the bed. (My children have always referred to me as "the bed Nazi" and steadfastly refuse to help me.) My grandmother's determination, exemplified during that afternoon while the wind blew furiously and tree limbs fell all around us, has given me the inner strength to face many challenges in my own life.

When she died in August of 1953, she had a huge funeral in Hartford and the news of her death was reported prominently in the Hartford Courant. After the service, the funeral cortege drove slowly from the synagogue past the old shul, which had opened its doors in her honor, and then past the Hebrew Home, where residents and staff came outside to stand in homage to her. I was pregnant when she died; four months later, when I had my first child, I named her Sarah Paula after my grandmother.

When I was growing up, the rabbi at the Emanuel Synagogue was Morris Silverman, who wrote a dozen prayer books that were used widely in the Conservative movement. His wife, Althea, was my mother's best friend. We called her Aunt Althea and my mother called her "Mrs. Rabbi." Rabbi Silverman married Bob and me in 1952. Years later, the Silvermans' older son, Hillel, ended his own very successful rabbinic career as the rabbi of Temple Sholom in Greenwich, Connecticut, a Conservative synagogue to which my daughter, Rachel, belongs. When Hillel Silverman delivered the eulogy at my mother's funeral in 2000, he talked about how my mother used to telephone his house when he was growing up. "It's Aunt Adeline," she would say. "Where's your mother?" He or his siblings would answer that she was busy or that it was Shabbos and she couldn't talk. "Put her on the phone!" my mother would order. "I need to talk to her." That was my mother, direct and outspoken.

My brother, sister and I didn't see a lot of our father, but he did appear periodically. Hermie Goldstein was short and chubby and had the most brilliant mind. He graduated from Yale Law School, where he had been my Uncle Eddie's roommate. His family, the Goldsteins, lived in West Hartford when I was born but moved to Yonkers when we were young. His sister, my aunt Gert, gave me piano lessons for some years.

Hermie and my mother always remained on very good terms. She loved him, but she couldn't live with him. He was a lawyer, but when he won a big case he would buy a new car instead of paying the bills. I think that was the basis for their divorce. I remember his coming to see us when he was in the chips, bringing incredible toys from FAO Schwarz. During the war, he became an entrepreneur, manufacturing parts for warplanes. He eventually developed the air purifier, though he didn't patent it, as well as 3D glasses. At the end of his life, he owned and ran Kilgen Organ in St. Louis.

When we were young, my father sometimes took us on vacations and my mother came too, though she stayed in a separate room with us. On one trip, we stayed at a cliff house hotel, where they were playing "Dancing Cheek to Cheek." Every time I hear that song, I remember climbing those long, steep steps. Another time, we traveled to Quebec to see the Dionne Quintuplets. Those poor quintuplets! I didn't realize it at the time, but they were kept on public display. We watched them from behind glass.

Hermie eventually remarried a lovely woman named Theodora, and they lived in New York in a gorgeous apartment on Park Avenue. I used to visit them when I was in college at Bryn Mawr. His wife was a Christian Scientist and died of cancer; she wouldn't accept any medical treatment. Right after Bob and I married, my father met us at the airport in New York before we flew to Mexico for our honeymoon. In later years, he would often take a small plane from LaGuardia Airport right to Worcester to visit us. He would get off the plane, the New York Times folded under his arm, the crossword puzzle completed in ink, and tease me that I hadn't been able to finish it. He only stayed the day, never longer. When our daughter, Sarah, was upset, he would sit at the piano and play for her by ear. He never knew a note, but he could play songs like, "When Peter Pumpkin Eater finds a wife and learns to keep her, I'll come back to you." Somewhere I have the notes for a song he wrote for me. When Sarah was really cranky, he would put her in the car with him – we didn't have car seats at the time – and take her for a ride to calm her down. One day, he appeared with one of those huge life-sized dolls just for her. She adored him.

My father's financial situation was precarious as he neared the end of his life, but he made sure that we weren't aware of his circumstances. One day when he was visiting us in

Worcester, he noticed the lot for sale directly behind our house on Salisbury Street. He told us, "You need to own that for the children to play." He immediately called Jack Wolfson, our friend and lawyer, and bought it for us as a present. A month later, the bank called and said we owed money. He never paid a cent himself for that land, but it was a brilliant decision!

My father once sent Bob tickets to go to the World Series. It wasn't until after he died that we found an entry in his diary that said, "Called Archie Katz in West Hartford. Asked him to send me money. Took a plane to New York, bought the tickets for Bob, left them for him and went back to St. Louis." He didn't want Bob to know he didn't have enough money on his own to buy him baseball tickets.

Gregarious and enthusiastic, my father always approached new people and new experiences with unbridled enthusiasm. It shouldn't have come as a surprise that his death in 1960 was as fascinating as his life. When he was living in New York, he had met and become dear friends with Helen Benitez, daughter of economist and civic leader Conrado Benitez; Helen herself served in the Philippine Senate. Hermie had become involved in a series of self-help projects to help impoverished Filipinos, focusing on health care, rural waterworks and distributing chicks to encourage poultry farming. For several years, he traveled repeatedly to the Philippines.

It was from Helen that I first received news that he had died of a heart attack; he was only 60. He had become such a revered figure in the Philippines that she asked if they could keep his body and have him lie in state before they returned him to the United States. My sister, brother and I gave our permission, and after a week we brought him back to the United States for a small funeral in New York.

After Helen called to tell us my father had died, Joel, Bob and I went down to New York so that we could tell my Uncle "Siggy," my father's brother, in person. The superintendant let us in the apartment he had shared with my father. He was sleeping, and before we woke him, we began to go through drawers to see if we could find my father's will. In his highboy, there was a drawer full of unopened bills and a summons from the government because he had not paid withholding taxes for the employees of the Kilgen Organ Company. In another drawer was the approval from the Small Business Administration for a government loan for some adventure he was on. And in a third drawer were his diaries. At that point, we woke up my uncle, who refused to believe that my father had died and began to scream at us to leave. (He suffered from some sort of mental illness.) I tossed the diaries, along with a small jade Buddha, into a zippered Grasshopper suitcase, and we left. That was my inheritance. I spent weeks afterwards going through everything to learn about the kind of man my father had been.

The estate wasn't even large enough to pay for the funeral. My brother and his wife, Diane, Bob and I, and my mother sat in the front row of the Frank E. Campbell Funeral Chapel on West 81st Street, a non-sectarian funeral home that was the only one we knew. Bob and Joel wanted to say goodbye to him, but I wouldn't go look in the coffin before they sealed it. The only other mourners were some people in the back row; they turned out to be people to whom my father owed money. There was a terrible snowstorm that day, and we were never able to see him buried because of the weather. I remember getting calls and letters from people my father hadn't paid. It broke my heart, but Bob and I didn't have much money ourselves. After awhile, Bob took those calls for me.

My son, David, was five when my father died; Sarah was seven. David once asked me why Grandpa Hermie hadn't lived with Grag, which was the nickname my children gave my mother. (When Sarah was little and tried to say "Grandma" it came out "Gragon" instead. The kids abbreviated it to "Grag." Bob was convinced it should have been "Dragon.") I wasn't sure how to explain the complications of divorce, so I told David, "My father had to go to Africa on business. And he couldn't come back for a long time. So he told my mother that it was okay for her to get married again." My son still talks about his grandfather who went off to Africa. He can't believe I spun that tale. Divorce wasn't an easy thing to discuss then, though it's difficult to believe now, when children routinely have different names from their parents, and there are so many varied types of families.

When I was eight years old, my mother also married again, a man named Harry Bishop, who was in his 40s and had been a confirmed bachelor. My sister, Jean, told my brother and me that Harry would behave like the stepmothers in the fairy tales if our mother married him. We had to get rid of him. So Joel and I, always gullible, would stand at the top of the big circular staircase when Harry brought my mother home. He always kissed her good night at the bottom of the stairs, right by the grandfather clock. And we would lean over the railing and spit at them. As soon as Harry left, my mother would come tearing up the stairs after us, and we would say, "Jean told us to do that!" My sister, reading a book on her bed, would look up, feigning surprise. "Mother, I don't know what they're talking about," she would say. "I never told them any such thing." Then off my mother would go with us to the playroom to punish us with the belt.

No matter how my mother treated me, I loved her dearly, and I did not want her to get married, especially when a friend told me that her father and mother slept in the same bed. Nonetheless, after a year's courtship, she married Harry in my Aunt Min's living room. Joel and I giggled during the ceremony; we were so nervous. From that point on, things were very different in our family.

It probably wasn't easy for Harry, a bachelor marrying into a household where there were three children and a strong-willed mother-in-law. But he was a difficult man, with a terrible temper and very little patience for us, especially where I was concerned. Harry hated my table manners, and he hated my practicing the piano. "Miss," he called me: "Miss, don't do that!" My mother never stood up for me. So, truth be told, I waited until I saw his car come into the driveway every evening, and then I sat down at the piano to practice. It was when Harry came into our lives that Joel began to clean my room for me so I wouldn't get into more trouble.

I moved from my former bedroom over the sun parlor to the middle room, right between my mother and Harry and my grandmother. Fran had married Sid Kaplan by then, and so Joel's bedroom was now upstairs on the third floor with Annie, where there were two bedrooms and a bath. He felt very far away to me.

It was the beginning of my learning to cope. I used to lie in my bed at night, listening to my mother and Harry fight about me. "You've got to do something about her!" he ranted to her, as though I was a tremendous problem that needed to be solved.

To drown out their voices, I did one of two things. I turned on the radio on my bedside table and listened to the Dodgers, my most favorite thing in the entire world. Or I rolled over in bed, pulled up the covers and lost myself by replaying the plot of a book or a movie in my head.

Divorce was unusual in those days, and I did my best to hide the fact that my mother and I had different last names. From the time she married Harry, when I was in the third grade, until we all legally changed our names from Goldstein to Bishop when I was twelve, I never invited her to come to anything that happened at school. If she heard about a parents' night or a program at school from Joel and asked me why I hadn't told her about it, I would say, "Oh, I forgot." I didn't want to have to introduce her to anybody with a name that was different from mine. Harry's presence sometimes made it difficult for me to understand my own father's role in my life. I remember sitting on the curb at Foxcroft Road with my brother, waiting for Hermie to come to see us. Once we sat there from early morning until dark, and he never came. Another time, he arrived when Harry also had tickets to take us to something. I sat on the porch in the hammock that day and cried, telling him, "I can't have two fathers!" And he got up and left.

I saw even less of my mother once she was married. I wanted her to love me, so I did very well in school, and I never told her when anything was troubling me. I tried to do the right thing. Even then my big mouth got me into trouble – it gets me into trouble to this day – but I never talked back to her. I was very careful.

Yet she continued to berate and criticize me, focusing in particular on my weight. She told me all the time how fat I was. It was true: I was always fat. It didn't stop me from eating – I loved to eat -- but I did hate being fat. It was especially difficult in school. Fat little kids always get picked last on a team, and nobody ever wanted me. When I was older, it was so embarrassing to have to put on my gym clothes in front of the other girls. When I went to college, I was mortified to wear a bathing suit. Interestingly, my mother herself had been heavy when she was young. (Indeed, I look exactly like her. I was always recognized as Adeline Bishop's daughter, especially when I was older and had my own young children with me.) Sometimes, I wonder if she was trying to protect me from the difficulties she endured, but she was so unkind that it is difficult to imagine her intentions as loving.

When I was eleven or so, we used to go downtown to shop at G. Fox and Company in Hartford because my mother had a close friend named Goldie who worked there. We called her "Aunt Goldie," just as we called all my mother's friends "aunt." At the department store, my mother would take me first to the Chubby Department, where she would tell everyone how fat I was and how terrible it was that I had to wear "chubby" clothes.

Not surprisingly, weight and dieting have always been an issue for me. Even when I was little, I remember lying in my bed saying to myself, "When I am very sick and dying, I will lose a lot of weight, and she will love me." When I was a teenager, I used to sneak food, hiding sandwiches and cookies in my dresser drawers and eating several candy bars when I went to the movies with my girlfriends. I suppose I was trying to punish my mother in some way. When I was twelve or thirteen, she and my Aunt Min took me to a fat farm for a couple of days. Aunt Min and I smuggled in candy bars in our pocketbooks.

As a child, I had a lot of funny little anxieties in addition to worrying about being fat. I was beside myself if I thought we were going to be late. We used to take the train from Hartford to Florida. I was a basket case, certain that we were going to miss the train, and so was my brother. Even when we were very small, the two of us would be dressed, sitting in the car ready to leave for the station, waiting for everyone else. I can still feel knots in my stomach if I'm running late. Yet part of that need for control was simple preservation; I taught myself certain coping skills that have been useful my entire life. Somehow, as a little child, I learned that the world wasn't such a dark place in the morning. So I could get into bed, think about the book I was reading, and go right to sleep. I still do that.

Books just transported me. I think I read every Nancy Drew and every Judy Bolton. I read books about people from every country – I had a set of those – and then I moved on to the Victorian novels: Jane Eyre, Wuthering Heights, Silas Marner, Vanity Fair. I found them delicious; they were an incredible escape. I remember reading Jane Eyre at the beach after services on Yom Kippur. We didn't eat, and I climbed up on my bed and read the book all day long. And of course I came down to dinner with big, red swollen eyes. I don't cry a lot in real life; I'm very self-possessed. But I sob in books or sad movies. In fact, I cried so at the end of the book I just finished reading – Moloka'i, by Alan Brennert -- that I was mortified. I was going out to dinner, and I had to keep putting Visine in my eyes and wear sunglasses.

I'm sure that my needing to read the end of a book before I began it stemmed from anxiety. Knowing how the story would turn out helped me exert control in a way I couldn't in my own life. I didn't always recognize the characters when I peeked at the ending of the Victorian novels I loved, but I needed to know that the heroine was all right. I always read the last chapter of Nancy Drew, too. Then, once I was sure of the finish, I started at the beginning. A few years ago, one of my grandchildren asked me to read Harry Potter. I couldn't get past the third in the series, but at some point I did go to Barnes and Noble, buy a cup of coffee and sit down to read the end of the very last Harry Potter so I would know how it came out, and I wouldn't have to worry anymore.

We had good times, too, no matter how complicated our lives were. There was a nice side of my stepfather, and I think he loved us in his own way. He used to make up funny stories and say funny things. He had a wonderful sense of humor. When I was sixteen, we went to court and Harry legally adopted Jean, Joel and me so that there could be no obstacle to our inheriting from him. (I remember asking the judge facetiously if I should sit on his lap, like in the movies.) Harry took us to Dodger games and to the movies, the circus and to Savin Rock Amusement Park in southern Connecticut. One memorable July, we had tickets to the Barnum and Bailey Circus in Hartford when Harry came in and said, "I've just gotten tickets to the Yankees-Indians game. What do you kids want to do? Do you want to go to the baseball game or to the circus?" Joel and I both said that we wanted to go see the Yankees play in the Bronx, and so we did. It was July 6, 1944, the day of the tragic circus fire in Hartford. When the tent began to burn, no one could escape; the cages of animals waiting to perform had blocked all of the entrances. Close to 170 people were killed and hundreds injured. If we had made a different choice that day, we all would have been among them.

If there was a sanctuary in my life, a place where I felt happy almost all of the time, it was the beach. Every summer, on the day school ended, my mother, my grandmother, Annie, the chauffeur and we three children packed up and left for Woodmont, a part of Milford in coastal Connecticut. Judy and her family also came. My grandmother owned a cottage there, where my mother, too, had grown up. We stayed at the beach all summer, until the day before school began in the fall. It was a constant, so engrained in the fabric of our lives that we even traveled during the summer of the polio scare, when it was against the law to move children from town to town. My mother put us on the floor of the car in the back and covered us with blankets.

We loved the beach. My brother and I slept out on a little closed-in porch. We lay on our stomachs with our feet in the air and looked out at the water and the seawall. I grew up listening to the sound of the waves. The name of our beach was Burwell Beach, nicknamed Rocky Beach, and we climbed all over the rocks. My brother had a sailboat, and there was a whole gang of kids. My Aunt Min and Uncle John had their own cottage five houses down from us. Aunt Min was a tough cookie, but we adored Uncle John. He was vice president and treasurer of the Hartford Courant. Many nights, the grownups all ate at our house, and we ate at their house with all the cousins. In between us lived my friend Beverly, who was older than I was. Across the street lived a friend of my mother's whom we called Aunt Kate. She once sewed an outfit for my doll, Boogie, and she had a son named Lionel, who was my friend. Another good friend was Dickie Jacobs, who still calls me every year on my birthday. We had cookouts and celebrated my Uncle John's birthday every Fourth of July. I have very little recollection of my sister there, but I do remember that she would come upstairs to go to bed at night and then sneak out to meet her friends. The stairs creaked, and Jean – she was really brilliant – figured out exactly where the creaks were so that she could slip downstairs without making a sound. One evening, she brought a boyfriend to dinner. It was the first time the family had met him. Before he arrived, she lectured us all about how we should behave. When we sat down for dinner, and he asked for someone to pass the corn, my uncle John picked up an ear and threw it at him. My sister nearly died of embarrassment.

My mother and grandmother used to send us just down the block to Allison's, one of those little corner grocery stores. We would cross the street and try to hide when we passed Aunt Min's house because she would always come outside and call, "Lois, while you're at Allison's ..." and ask me to pick up whatever she needed, too. That was the story of my life: "Lois, while you're at Allison's...." We also used to go to Sloppy Joe's on the corner, where you could get steak sandwiches and hot dogs and razz limes. My mother and Aunt Min loved the egg creams, and we would bring them back a huge pitcher. Across the street was a little stand that sold bubble gum and, down the way, a little fish market on the next beach, Sandy Beach.

My mother and my aunt fought like cats and dogs, but every afternoon they would call to each other, "what time are you going swimming?" At the appointed time, my aunt would walk out to the beach in front of her house, and my mother would walk out to the beach in front of our house, and they would swim together, each in front of her own house.

Every fall, we returned to the beach for the High Holidays, attending services at a little Orthodox shul. It was quiet then, with few if any other summer people, and the sun went down much earlier than in the summer. My mother and grandmother would still send us to Allison's, and often my sister would go with me. We would begin to walk in the dark, and Jean would say, "I'm a witch and I'm going to scare you." I would scream all the way to the store, grab what we needed and cry all the way home. The next time my grandmother asked me to go, I would say, "Jean, you can't come with me." She always promised not to scare me. And then as soon as we stepped outside of the house, she would leer at me and say in a quiet, menacing voice, "The witch has come back." No wonder I'm easily frightened.

We all loved the beach, but my mother remained as strict as ever. On a day when she was recuperating from gall bladder surgery, I borrowed an inner tube from someone and went out in the water. I kept losing the tube on the waves, and because it wasn't mine, I followed it out. I couldn't make it back to shore. Without realizing who I was, my aunt saw my bathing cap bobbing in the waves and said to her babysitter, a young college boy, "that little girl is in trouble." She sent him out in the rowboat to rescue me. I couldn't make it to the boat, and he had to jump into the water and pull me up. I came home chilled and frightened, but it was my Aunt Fran who wrapped me up and comforted me. My mother punished me, putting me to bed and leaving me there.

Another example of my mother's discipline has stayed with me all these years. I hated summer squash as a child, but we often had it anyway, sitting down together at the dining room table in Milford for a big noon meal with my grandmother. One day, I wouldn't eat my squash, and she sent me up to my room. I had to stay there the entire day. At dinnertime, when, at last, I was allowed to come downstairs, there was the squash, waiting for me at my place at the table.

As I grew older, it became more rather than less difficult to be happy in our house. Jean went to a private day school called Chaffee and was out of the house with her friends all the time. My brother went to a private school in Simsbury, Connecticut, where he stayed overnight during the week. About this time, my grandmother had a severe nervous breakdown. Indeed, she was the oldest person who had ever had a frontal lobotomy. Though I was young and not very knowledgeable about such things, it seemed that the lobotomy was successful. I never noticed any pronounced differences in her personality because of it. A few years later, not long before she died, she came to my wedding and wanted to march down the aisle after me; clearly, she remained pretty feisty.

At the time of her breakdown, however, my grandmother used to scream at my mother, and so of course my mother left the house as often as she could. With the strain, my mother's terrible migraines worsened. I remember her sitting up in a chair in her darkened bedroom for two days at a time. I often had to soothe my grandmother when she was yelling. Although there was an aide to help, I was virtually alone in the house.

Every Friday, I climbed onto my bicycle, plopped a little red fake alligator bag into the basket, and escaped to Fran and Sid's for the weekend. They had bought a house not far from where we lived, and I spent almost every weekend with them. I babysat for their daughter, Judy, so they could go out. I don't think there ever was a question in my mind about why I went there. I hated being at home. I loathed my stepfather. My grandmother was both domineering and ill. And my mother was always yelling, because there was always something that we were doing wrong. So I used to get on my bike and go to Fran's. It was a family there, and I was part of it. I was loved. As soon as I was old enough, I packed my trunk and left Foxcroft Road for boarding school.

CHAPTER TWO

I WANT TO
BE SOMEBODY

"To Lois Bishop, Dear advisor,
Kindly leave my daughter wiser;
That she may live in placid bliss,
Advise her not to write like this."

- Ogden Nash

Drew Seminary for Young Women was in Carmel, New York, 80 miles from Hartford and a million miles away from the stresses and strains of my childhood. It had been founded in the mid-nineteenth century by railroad speculator Daniel Drew, who grew up in Carmel and also contributed to Drew Theological Seminary in New Jersey (now part of Drew University). My Drew was a four-year preparatory school for girls, a small institution of only one hundred and fifty or so, and it showed me a world where I knew I could matter.

Despite the constraints of my life at home, I had become more of an extrovert as I grew older and developed more self-confidence. Nobody had ever considered me funny, but I gradually learned that I had a good sense of humor and that I was able to make people laugh. I had chosen to attend Drew because I hadn't been accepted at Chaffee, my sister's school. But it soon didn't matter. At Drew, I made many friends, including Bobbie Bernstein, whom I discovered again years later in Sarasota by recognizing her picture in the newspaper. My best friend at Drew, Janet Clark, lived near me in West Hartford. We used to travel back and forth to school together. I don't think I made the connection then, but I remember getting on the bus with my girlfriend, so glad to be going back – and leaving Hartford behind.

I put on a lot of pounds when I was a freshman, but in four years at prep school I don't remember anyone ever commenting on my weight. I was never picked on. I loved being part of a group; I still find considerable support in that kind of belonging. As at most girls' schools, we had countless traditions. I sang in the Glee Club and belonged to one of the three sororities, or clubs, that were open to all juniors and seniors. We wore hats and gloves. When I was a freshman, I even had a crush on the senior who was my big sister. We went to dances at Peekskill Academy and the Hotchkiss School and invited boys to our place for dances.

At Drew, for the first time, I had teachers who really pushed me, especially an English teacher named Miss Crowley. I also liked Latin, which I took for four years. I was very self-motivated and competitive. Indeed, I eventually graduated as valedictorian of my class, after a hard-won battle for the honor with another classmate. I had always read a great deal, but at prep school I read almost constantly.

We did everything in a group. Once a year, we went by bus to see an opera at the Metropolitan. During my four years at Drew, I saw "Aida," "Tannhauser," "Lohengrin," and "Carmen." A music appreciation class, as well as our trips to the city, showed me how much I loved music, and I learned to escape into symphonies. I never developed highbrow taste; I have always liked Tchaikovsky and Beethoven.

I was glad to be away from home, but occasionally my mother reached out to me. In the fall of 1947, she called the headmistress to release me from school, telling her, "Lois has a doctor's appointment at Gate 3." I went into New York regularly to see a doctor for my eczema, so my mother often made such calls. But this time the Dodgers were in the World Series, and I knew from the coded message that she – or my stepfather, Harry -- had tickets to the game. I got on the train and went down to New York and met my family at Gate 3 at Yankees Stadium. It was the most exciting day. When I came back to Drew, the headmistress asked, "How was your doctor's appointment?"

I have always thrived on structure, and Drew was no different. Frankly, I think that's why I have always liked school. A school setting brought established tasks, rules and hours. There was little left to chance. From the time I was young until today, I have found the formlessness of Sundays daunting. When I had young children, I didn't like the absence of routine, with no set time for meals or activities. Without scheduled classes, Sundays were lonesome at prep school and in college, too, but at Drew at least we were expected to go to church. If your church wasn't nearby – and there was certainly no synagogue in Carmel, New York in the 1940s – you had to go to the Methodist Church, with which Drew was affiliated. I spent four years attending chapel every morning, church every Sunday morning and vespers every Sunday afternoon. I knew every hymn in the hymnal, and I loved them all. When I met Bob, he couldn't bear it when a hymn would come on the radio in the car, and I would bellow along. It didn't mean that I felt any less Jewish. I just liked the hymns. And I welcomed the order that church imposed on the week when I was at school.

Exercise was mandatory, and every morning after breakfast, no matter what the weather, we had to walk a rocky path up and around a big hill past the President's House. In addition, when we were punished, we had to walk extra laps. There were a lot of rules – silly rules, many of them -- and at prep school, rules were meant to be broken. I wasn't very brave, but I did occasionally venture into uncharted territory. We often sneaked out of our rooms at night, after lights out. In particular, we used to slip down the hall to hang out in the room of a popular teacher. (I didn't know that she was gay, but when it was later discovered, she was forced to leave the school.) One cold spring day, I was marching around the path, fuming that I had been punished for a minor infraction. As I did my assigned laps, I vowed that one day I would become very famous and everybody would know me. I look back on that moment as a turning point in my life. It was just the barest articulation, a teenager's inchoate dream, but it revealed the sense of purpose that would propel me through one door after another as I grew up.

World War II defined my early adolescence, both at home and during my first year at Drew. As in so many lives, it began for us with an interruption. Late on a Sunday afternoon, my mother had company, and I went upstairs to my room to listen to "The Shadow" on the radio. I couldn't find the station. I came running downstairs, saying, "Mom, something's going on, I can't find 'The Shadow.'" She turned on the radio to show me where it was and that was how we learned about the war. It was December 7, 1941. The next day, we gathered around the radio, listening to Franklin Roosevelt's speech to Congress. He was our biggest hero. It was a time when the radio was a centerpiece in every home. Every Sunday night, we sat in the living room, listening to Jack Benny and George Burns together. For the next four years, we followed developments overseas that same way, tracking the news and listening to the President's updates on Allied victories and defeats.

I was eleven when the war started – and it was a scary time. My cousin, Michael Sudarsky, went to war and so did his friends. I knew somebody who was killed. Rationing was strict. My stepfather, Harry, was an air warden, responsible for enforcing the blackouts. I remember D-Day, and I remember when the Japanese surrendered and there was dancing in the streets. By that time, I was fifteen. We were at the beach that August, and my brother and I went out celebrating.

Virtually the only negative experience I had at Drew that I recall occurred near the end of the war, in the spring of my freshman year. I had gone into New York City for my regular eczema shot and was walking up the hill toward school from the train station when I heard someone shout from an open window: "Ha! Your president died!" It was April 12, 1945, the day that Franklin Roosevelt died. I was beside myself; he had been my hero. Yet someone else was happy about his death because he was a Democrat.

Every summer, I returned home from Drew and found a job. One summer, I worked in the dry goods department at Brown Thompson, a local department store in Hartford. Once, when someone ordered a yard of material, I pulled the cloth off the bolt and took out my scissors. But when I made the first cut and tore it, it ripped the wrong way, down instead of across, and I was hysterical. One of the older women working there said, "Come with me," and took me into the back room. Here there was a hidden box where the saleswomen put their mistakes. I stuffed my ruined effort into the box and thanked her for protecting me.

Another summer, I worked for a camp in Hartford that was run by the Fresh Air Fund. Before the children got on the bus every morning, we had to check to make sure they didn't have lice. I had friends among the counselors, and by that time I was 17 and could go out at night. I had wonderful boy cousins who were my brother's age, and we all went out together. I had my first boyfriend, an older boy named Billy Hoffman who went to Syracuse. He invited me to visit for a weekend, and my mother wouldn't let me go. I carried on, crying and accusing her of being unfair, but of course she was absolutely right.

In the spring of 1948, I graduated at the top of my class at Drew and delivered the valedictory address. My years at Drew had been really happy ones for me. As I look back now, I realize that it was because, at last, I could be who I really was. Away from my mother's criticism, my stepfather's anger and my grandmother's mental illness, I blossomed.

That sense of freedom only deepened at Bryn Mawr, where I followed my sister, Jean. From the first day until I graduated,

I knew that I could achieve anything in the world as long as I was capable. An incident that occurred on my second day on campus immediately boosted my confidence. I had arrived in my dormitory for freshman week to discover that many of my classmates already knew each other from prep school. There were upperclassmen who had come back early to welcome us, but at first I felt isolated and uncomfortable. Then, on the second day, I had to pick up a form in Taylor Hall, the administration building. I came into the building and ran up the stairs. As I neared the top, an incredibly tall, thin and elegant woman came out into the hallway from her office. It was Katharine E. McBride, the President of the College. She had a stature that was absolutely ramrod. She looked down at me and said, "That's what I like to see, Miss Bishop: a lot of energy." I was overwhelmed. I think I squeaked "Thank you!" and went on. But I said to myself, "the President of Bryn Mawr College knows who I am! So I *am* somebody!" That moment, which I still remember exactly, set the tone for my college career.

Bryn Mawr was warm and enveloping, an environment that nurtured and sustained its students. There couldn't have been more than 500 of us in the undergraduate college, in addition to the very small graduate program. Even as freshmen, we always had full professors rather than teaching assistants. I would walk across the campus, and somebody would always say, "Hi, Lois, how's it going?" or "How are you, Miss Bishop?" I loved it, and I succeeded there, though my academic work sometimes left something to be desired. I asked for the least scientific course available to fulfill my science requirement and ended up in Geology. I was thrilled because the professor, Dr. Watson, had married a student, and he was gorgeous; perhaps there was hope for me. I loved taking Geology. During the first semester, I enjoyed learning about dinosaurs, and I liked looking for fossils. During the second semester, however, we had to use a microscope. Dr. Watson would stand over me and exclaim, "What do you mean, you can't see anything?" At the end of the year, he looked at me and said, "Miss Bishop, I should never pass you, but the thought of you in my class for another year would be more than I could bear." That's how I completed my science requirement. I ended up majoring in English Literature by default. By the time I thought I might like Sociology, it was too late; I had many more English credits.

I made a lot of good friends in college, particularly in my dormitory, Pembroke (or Pem) West. I am still very close to my friend, Lois Gordon, whom I met our first year. I introduced her to my cousin, Danny, and they got married, though it later ended in divorce. We reconnected many years later and have taken wonderful trips together. As a freshman, I became very friendly with a group of juniors, who used to call me their mascot. Three of them came from Boston and invited me to come visit them during Christmas vacation. Before we left school, however, one of them said to me, "Lois, I want to warn you before you come that my parents may say some terrible things about the Jews." I remember saying, "I cannot stay at your house." I did meet my friends there (I stayed with one of the others), and I had a wonderful time. One of them had an illegal car –we weren't supposed to have cars at school – and so she would drive us home. They were so supportive and loving of me, giving me the nurturing I had never received at home.

I didn't have a lot of spending money; in fact, I don't believe I had much of any. I worked whenever I could. I was the fire warden in my dorm. Everybody would watch to see what time I went to bed in case there was going to be a fire drill, so I had to go to sleep and set my alarm clock. I ran the little hall shop, open from eight to nine pm. at night, where you could buy candy bars, personal goods, Kleenex and odds and ends like that. And, for a long time, I also worked for a catalogue company on Saturday mornings, sorting product sheets into envelopes. In my inimitable need to organize the world, I tried different ways of collating to be more efficient. I also babysat, especially for Dean Marshall, the Dean of Students, with whom I developed a wonderful relationship. She was very kind, a real mentor to me.

In my junior year, I became a freshman advisor, and one of my advisees was Isabelle Nash, the daughter of Ogden Nash. She gave me a book of her father's poetry that he inscribed to me. I was also Hall President of Pem West in my senior year. When there were concerns about students in the dorm, Dean Marshall would call me over to meet with the administration; they would share confidential information with me, asking me to keep an eye on the situation. Their trust in me, allowing me to handle problems knowing that I wouldn't tell tales, was very important to me.

Just as at Drew, there were many traditions at Bryn Mawr, traditions that enveloped me. We sang in Greek; we danced around the May Pole. During freshman week, we received our light blue lanterns. In October, there was a special day where all the upperclassmen gave the freshmen presents. I was Senior Song Mistress my final year, responsible for leading the singing. I loved the experience. Over the library door was a statue of Athena, the goddess of wisdom, with an owl on her shoulder. The owl was the college mascot. I began to collect owls, a hobby that has lasted over sixty years.

In January of my sophomore year, I received a telephone call from a man named Bob Green, who was getting his MBA at the Wharton School at the University of Pennsylvania. He had gotten my name from a mutual friend, Norman Asher, whom I had met the summer before when he was clerking for his uncle in Hartford. Norman had written to Bob suggesting that he might want to look me up. I was nothing special, Norman warned him, but he might very well be able to meet somebody cute through me.

Bob Green and I had a long conversation on the phone and agreed to meet. He told me his car was being fixed, and so I planned to take the Paoli Local that went from Bryn Mawr into 30th Street Station in Philadelphia. It was cold that January, and I wore a fur coat that made me look even larger than my heavy self. I had told him what I was going to wear, but he never described himself. He always remarked afterwards that he had seen me from a distance – this fat little person in a big fur coat -- and tried to make up his mind whether to approach me or just turn around and leave. He did come up to me, and we went out for dinner and to a basketball game at Penn. At the end of the evening, I climbed back onto the Paoli Local to return to Bryn Mawr. After I sat down, I turned to some women I knew who had also been in Philadelphia that evening and said, "I just met the man I'm going to marry." And that was the beginning of it.

Bob was five years older than I, born in 1925, and raised in Worcester, Massachusetts, the son of Irving and Belle Green. He had enlisted in the army at the age of 18 and served in France until he was wounded – shot in the face – in November of 1944. By the time I met him, he had undergone considerable surgery and rehabilitation, spending over a year in an army hospital at Stanford University. The GI Bill had enabled him to go to college at Clark University and then on to Wharton for business school.

He never had any money; in fact, he told me his car was in the shop for three months before I finally realized he didn't have a car at all! And so he used to take the train to Bryn Mawr on the weekends. (He never stayed overnight. Men were not allowed in the rooms after six p.m.) I told him how to get from Philadelphia to Bryn Mawr by teaching him the acronym that named the stops -- Old Maids Never Wed and Have Babies -- for Overbrook, Marion, Narberth, Wynwood, Ardmore, Haverford, Bryn Mawr. He would mutter the names of the towns to himself all the way out from Philadelphia.

Everybody knew Bob. He was fun and funny; he even had a part in our junior show. His being a part of my Bryn Mawr experience just made it all the more wonderful. Some people had boyfriends and were never involved in campus life because they were off with their boyfriends. But Bob was there all the time. He never separated me from the school. He just became a part of it with me.

We once made a big bet when he told me his mother used to make chopped liver with calves' liver. "Nobody makes chopped liver with calves' liver!" I said. "Everybody makes it with chicken livers." That was the first time I spoke to his mother on the telephone. I lost the bet, and I had to treat him to a big, fancy dinner.

The summer after I met Bob, I went to Europe. Before meeting my sister in Switzerland, I was going to tour Italy for Holy Year of Jubilee. My mother made reservations for me to join a tour group, and it wasn't until I met the group in Paris that I learned they were all priests and nuns. I thought to myself, "Oh, my God, wait till they find out I'm Jewish." I couldn't sleep. I kept trying to figure out how I was going to tell them. And then, on the first Sunday morning together, we were having breakfast and they said, "Lois, dear, what are you going to do while we're at church?" So they all knew in advance, and they were wonderful. I even had a brief romance with a young man who was about to enter the seminary.

We traveled all over and had an audience with Pope Pius XII. We stood right up at the rope that separated the group from him, but I moved back because I thought it would mean more to the others to be so close to him. I never forgot how the Pope spoke to each group of pilgrims in their own language. I remember standing in St. Peter's Cathedral and saying to myself, "what is this little girl doing in St. Peter's, having an audience with the Pope?" I think I had a papal blessing, which I hope has carried me through my life.

We drove over the Italian Alps, and then the tour group left me in Zurich, where my sister lived with her Norwegian husband, Pelle. Jean had met Pelle when they were both in school at the University of Zurich. Jean had been studying German during her junior year abroad from Bryn Mawr, and Pelle was studying to be a pediatrician. When Jean returned home after that year, my mother wouldn't speak to her because she had fallen in love with a non-Jew. Mother refused to give her any money for her senior year at Bryn Mawr, hoping that she would change her mind. My grandmother, on the other hand, was wonderful when Pelle came to visit. She was warm and loving to him, and Bob and I both loved him. Ultimately, he and Jean were married in Europe and then went to Boston, where he had a residency. They were divorced many years ago, and he long since returned to Norway. I know she still stays in close contact with his nieces and nephews. Jean herself has a Ph.D. in history and was a professor of ancient and medieval history at the University of Wisconsin at Lacrosse for many, many years.

The summer I went to Europe, I stayed with my sister and brother-in-law for a while, and then Jean and I traveled all over Europe together. I remember spending the night in a flea-bitten hotel in Belgium and scratching all night. We went on to Copenhagen and then to Oslo, where I met Pelle's family. They were simply wonderful and just opened their arms to me. I stayed two weeks and became very attached to his mother, in particular. It was an interesting family. During World War II, when the Nazis invaded Norway, Pelle's parents had left in the middle of the night and crossed over the mountains to Sweden, a neutral country. My brother-in-law wasn't with them. He and his friends had been caught listening to the BBC broadcasts from England, which was illegal. He was sent to a concentration camp, though, as a Norwegian, he wasn't poorly treated. But he saw what happened to the Jews.

That was a wonderful and eye-opening summer for me. Bob wrote me every day. (I still have his letters.) He was working as a camp counselor and had terrible hay fever. Every day, he sat in the middle of a lake in a boat and wrote me letters. When I came back, he and I were together for the rest of my junior year at Bryn Mawr. When he graduated from Wharton that spring, I went back to Worcester with him, and he took me to get my engagement ring. During my senior year, he often had to cancel his plans to visit me in Philadelphia because he hadn't made enough money that week to travel.

The first time I brought Bob home to introduce him to my family, my mother said to him, "How could you have fallen in love with her? She's so fat!" He was furious. I don't remember turning my back on her, but Bob told me that for a year after we married and moved to Worcester, I wouldn't go to Hartford or talk to my mother on the telephone. I have no recollection of her visiting us until Sarah was born, and she came to stay with us for a while to help me.

My grandmother, in contrast, was as welcoming and loving to Bob as she had been to my sister's husband, Pelle. After we were engaged, she once asked him, "Bob, do you have a navy blue suit?" He said, "No, I don't." And she opened up her little clasp purse and took out $100 – I can't imagine what that would be today – and handed it to him so he could buy himself a suit and go to functions properly dressed. He went to Ware Pratt Co., which used to be at the corner of Main and Pearl Streets in downtown Worcester, and bought a suit, some shirts, a pair of shoes, ties -- all for a hundred dollars.

I graduated from Bryn Mawr in May of 1952. To this day, I know that part of who I am today is because I went to a women's college, particularly one as supportive as Bryn Mawr. It was an extraordinary experience to spend four years on a campus where professors said hello to me, the Dean of the College was my mentor, and the President knew my name. It kept reinforcing my belief that I was somebody. That fat little girl deep inside of me developed a sense of self-worth, a conviction that I had value. In combination, prep school and college made me realize that I could do whatever I wanted. The opposite simply never occurred to me.

Bob and I were married on June 30, just a few weeks after my graduation. My mother gave me money for furniture for our house instead of a big wedding. We couldn't get the country club on a Sunday, so we were married on a Monday at two o'clock in the afternoon. Bob always joked that we did that to make it difficult for any of his family to come to our wedding.

In December, six months after we were married, my Aunt Eddy and Uncle Eddie asked us if we wanted to drive their car down to Boca Raton. They would pay for our expenses on the way down as well as our plane tickets home. We were so excited and jumped at the opportunity because we could then go on to Miami and visit my grandmother. We decided to take my cousin Judy with us. She was eleven years old. It was her first trip away from home, and she cried during the two nights we spent on the road. She quickly adjusted.

We arrived in Boca, and then my aunt and uncle drove us to my grandmother's house, where we spent a wonderful few days. One evening, my grandmother gave us $100 to go out by ourselves. That amused us because during the day she made us go from store to store to find oranges that were a few pennies cheaper. By the time we returned home to Massachusetts, we realized we had more money than when we had left!

In Worcester, I went to work at the Clark University library, making $30 a week. My job was filing journals. I had a blast. The seniors were only a year younger than I was, so I would sneak out and have coffee with them. Miss Henderson, the librarian, wasn't always very happy with me. After a few months, Bob asked if I would come to work for him. He had started a little insurance brokerage agency supported by Hy and Lou Small, who had a large agency. I didn't find it very fulfilling because I couldn't stand the way Bob did things. His personality was so laid-back. I knew there was a better system than his, and I itched to reorganize the office and his clients. But I managed for about nine months and then I got pregnant with Sarah. And that was my early working experience.

I loved working, but I wanted a child. Sarah was born on December 23, 1953 and named after my grandmother, who had died several months before. We were still living at Salisbury Gardens then, paying only $82 a month in rent. In 1955, on Halloween, we moved to 2 Rutland Terrace, and David was born a little over a month later, on December 9th. My mother had taken Sarah back to Hartford with her in preparation for the new baby's birth. Bob drove me to the hospital and then went home to wait. He was sleeping when my obstetrician called to tell him he was about to deliver the baby. "You go right ahead," said Bob, and turned over to go back to sleep, thinking the doctor had only called to ask his permission. Then he realized what he had actually heard, jumped out of bed and raced to the hospital. We named the baby David Edward for Bob's grandfather. David was sick with a bacterial infection when he was two. We kept him at home as our pediatrician suggested instead of treating him in the hospital. Dr. Edmund Piehler made a house call every morning to check on him, but it was a year before he fully recovered.

The night Patty was born, on May 20, 1960, I was at a board meeting at the Jewish Community Center. I knew I was in labor, but I didn't want to create a scene by leaving the meeting early. I sat there with a piece of paper, jotting down the names of girls.

(We already had boys' names picked out.) After the meeting, I came home and said to Bob, "I'm jumping in the shower; I'm going to have a baby." He was watching television, and he said, "Get out of my way, I can't see the screen."

Right after delivery, when I was still mostly sedated, Bob asked me if I had picked out a name. I sat straight up and said, "It's Patricia Ruth, and I don't want to discuss it further."

Later, I woke to hear Bob telling me the baby's name.

"Patricia Ruth?" I said to Bob. "Where did you get that name? I wanted Rachel or Rebecca."

"You told me that was her name," he said. "You can't change it now. The kids have already gone to school to tell all of their friends that they have a new baby sister, and her name is Patricia Ruth."

When I finally absorbed this information, we had to decide for whom to name her. She was named for my father's sister, my Aunt Gert, whose Hebrew name was Gittel. Patty has refused ever to be called Patricia, only Patty.

Two years later, when I was pregnant with Rachel, we were in the process of building an addition to the house, a huge addition with more square footage than the original house. We lived in it during construction, and everything was filthy, with soot and sawdust everywhere. Bob and I occasionally had to sleep on the living room floor. One day, the kids came in with their friends and started to play Tic, Tac, Toe in the dust on the furniture. I had had it. I picked up a table to move it, and my water broke. It was a month early. "I won't move," I promised Dr. Albert Jones, who insisted that I go to the hospital. "You have to come in," he told me. "There is too great a chance of infection." Rachel was born on April 9, 1962. She was named Rachel because I loved that name; her second name, Elizabeth, was probably for my stepfather Harry's mother, Ethel.

Bob, who hadn't been in the delivery room for the births of the other children, decided he wanted to watch Rachel's birth. It was during the playoffs for the Masters golf tournament, and he and Dr. Jones watched the match in the doctors' lounge on the floor. They were so involved that by the time they finally paid attention to me, it was too late for Bob to change into scrubs. He ended up having to watch through the glass.

Dr. Jones lifted the baby up so he could see, and Bob put his thumb up. He had a baby boy. Now he would have two boys and two girls. When the doctor came out of the delivery room, he said, "Congratulations, Bob. You have a lovely baby girl."

"Dr. Jones," Bob said. "That was a baby boy."

"That was the umbilical cord, Bob," the doctor told him. "Why don't you stick to the insurance business and I'll stick to delivering babies?"

I can't imagine what would have happened if he had already called our parents.

It was a different world then. We left our doors unlocked, the children walked back and forth to school, and we knew all the neighbors. We had block parties and went caroling every December; they still carol together in the Rutland Terrace neighborhood. I loved the caroling, just as I had loved the hymns when I was a student at Drew. I was a nice Jewish girl, and yet I knew the words to all the carols. There were always kids in my house, playing in the backyard or selling lemonade. That's what children did after school. They brought their friends home, or they played in the neighborhood. On nice days in the spring or fall, they could be outside all day without checking in with me; the only rule was that they had to be home by dark. If I were late coming home myself, I only had to call one of the neighbors, and she would look out for my children.

When the children were small, an elderly gentleman and his daughter lived next door to us. They sold the house when I was pregnant with Rachel. When the new people arrived, a station wagon drove up and out came the Petters: three little girls and their mother, who was pregnant. Talk about luck! Rachel and Caroline Petter were born at almost the same time, and then there were four girls exactly my children's ages living right next door. (David had a good friend across the street.) We would take turns watching each other's children.

The two babies spent a lot of time in the playpen together. They were inseparable growing up. One afternoon when the little girls were about four or five, I was going through the toys in Rachel and Patty's room. The doorbell rang. I came down, and Betty Petter was standing there.

"What are you doing?" She was a little annoyed.

"What do you mean, 'what am I doing?'" I answered. "I'm cleaning out the broken toys."

She said, "Lois, the two girls are going into your discards and bringing everything upstairs in my house to Caroline's room!"

We laughed. Here they were walking in with puzzle pieces and bits of old toys, and she thought I had given it all to them.

It was that kind of a relationship. We weren't socially friendly, but we helped each other out. Patty and Rachel, who were closest to the Petter girls, loved going over there for dinner.

They would come home and I would ask, "What did you have for dinner?"

And they would say, "Oh, we had a remembrance meal."

"What's a remembrance meal?"

"Remember when we had ham on Monday night? Remember when we had meatloaf on Wednesday night?"

They thought that was wonderful. I would say, "How come you're eating things there that you wouldn't touch here?" "But it was a remembrance meal!" they would say.

My children all went to Lee Street School, at the corner of Lee Street and Institute Road. It later became a Head Start school and then a public health building; it is now part of Worcester Polytechnic Institute. It was a very small school, with only one class and a single teacher for every grade. The children used to come home for lunch every day. The Callahan family lived a block away, on Massachusetts Avenue. All four of my children were the same ages as four of theirs. My children would pick the Callahans up on the way to school. Rachel would give the weather report for the day or announce what I was doing. Sid Callahan used to say she learned everything she needed to know about us from the morning report on the way to school.

There weren't a lot of Jewish children at Lee Street, and Sarah had particularly unhappy experiences there. When she was five years old, she walked home from school and said, "I would rather be Christmas than Jewish." David had some Jewish classmates, and so he was fine.

I was always involved in what my children were doing. I was active in the PTA at Lee Street, which was so small that parents played a significant role in the life of the school. I did everything but bake. Every time they asked mothers to bake, I sent in Oreos. Kids liked Oreos! It was a treat for them. One day, my own children said, "Mom, why don't you just send in a couple of dollars?" And that was the end of my Oreos.

From the moment Bob and I had married and moved to Worcester, we had a ready group of friends, Bob's best friends from childhood, the Sadowskys, Wolfsons and Rudnicks. Two of the wives, Barbara Rudnick (now Greenberg) and Joan Sadowsky, were also from out of town, and I became friends with them; they are still my best friends. Both had been married longer than I had and already had children. From the very start, I was in a warm, secure place. I loved my husband and my home; I had new friends and, within a year, a new baby I adored. Had I been anybody else, I would have been totally happy.

But I wasn't. We used to go to friends' houses on Saturday nights for potluck suppers. After dinner, the women would sit around in the kitchen and talk about babies and recipes. I would sit there and think, "Oh, my God, this has got to be the most boring conversation." I'd get up and walk into the living room, and there the men would be, discussing politics. The media at the time was filled with images of the good housewife, how important it was to have cleaner, whiter sheets than your next-door neighbor. That was the environment. I said to myself, "Here I am with a wonderful college education, and I am in the kitchen cooking and washing clothes and changing diapers." I took my Bryn Mawr diploma and had it framed for $30 – probably the equivalent of $150 today – and hung it over my washing machine.

In the late 1960s, Peggy Lee recorded a song with the refrain, "Is that all there is?" And those words captured the way I felt as a young housewife. I knew there was something else for me. I just had to figure out what it was.

CHAPTER THREE

IS THAT ALL THERE IS?

*"Had we known, in that kingdom of night, that you knew and
did nothing, we would have all died of despair."*

Elie Wiesel

Caught within the domestic parameters of the fifties
housewife, I didn't know what I wanted, but I knew I
wasn't content. My first opportunity to *do* something came
through community involvement, initially in the women's
organizations in the Jewish community. Bob and I had both
been raised and married in a Conservative synagogue, but
when I moved to Worcester, I soon discovered that men and
women didn't sit together at Congregation Beth Israel, the
local Conservative synagogue. I remember saying to Bob, "I
will not be a member of some place where I can't sit with you."
I refused to be relegated to a separate section because I was

a woman. That self-assertion was a key part of my identity, a legacy of having been raised by strong and independent women, particularly my grandmother. Nobody else thought the way I did. At that time, I was quite isolated in my understanding of women's roles and capabilities. So I put my foot down, and we joined Temple Emanuel. Bob's parents weren't too happy, and neither were mine. But Temple turned out to be very traditional; it was about as Conservative as my synagogue in Hartford. Children went to Hebrew school three days a week, and congregants wore *tallitot* and *yarmulkes*, so I felt fine there. Indeed, some of my friends left to start Temple Sinai because they thought that Temple Emanuel was too conservative.

With over a thousand families in the congregation at that time, High Holiday services were held in Memorial Auditorium in Lincoln Square. Seating was assigned according to social and family connections, longevity and financial means. Our tickets, of course, were for seats way in the back. I loved to sing, and so at services I sang as loudly as I could. One day I went in and sat down, and the person in the row ahead of me said, "Well, here comes the singer again." So I wrote a letter to the Board of Trustees and asked, "Would you please move my seat? I don't care where you move me, but I like to sing, and the congregants around me make fun of me." The following year, our tickets were for seats all the way up in the front! Bob and I ended up sitting with the important people only because I opened my big mouth.

I was in my early twenties when I became involved in the Temple Sisterhood. I knew Anita Robbins, who was president, and there were other women, such as Gladys Silverman, who mentored those of us who were young. Gladys held cooking classes for the young brides. Bob was also involved in Temple activities. Lew Wald, who was Temple president in the 1960s, inaugurated a wonderful young leadership program, taking young men with leadership potential and training them. For Bob, that program began his long commitment to Temple, where he ultimately served as president from 1973 to 1977. Lew Wald was way ahead of his time in recognizing the need to train young leaders, but it was the men he singled out. I felt rebuffed. Here my husband was making a difference at a leadership level and I was "just" in Sisterhood. I wasn't interested in centerpieces; I wasn't interested in cooking. I never passed judgment on the other women, for they were whipping up these things with no trouble, and I wouldn't even have known how to begin. But just as I was drawn away from the women's homey chitchat towards the men's political debates at our potluck suppers, so did I know that I wanted to do more than serve as part of the domestic arm of Temple Emanuel.

During that time, in the mid-fifties, I joined and participated in the local chapters of the National Council of Jewish Women as well as Women's American ORT. By 1959, when I was 29, I had joined the board of the Jewish Community Center (JCC). I also became secretary of the Worcester Jewish Federation. Sitting at the head table as secretary, I would watch as the president signaled a friend in one of the front rows to table a motion or adjourn the meeting if deliberations weren't proceeding to his satisfaction. I was learning how the big boys did it. Even then, I realized that, as a woman, I had skills that were different from the men's. Nonetheless, observing how they operated gave me quite an education. Moreover, I also figured out quite early that I had very little tolerance for wasting energy on inconsequential matters. In the mid-1960s, for example, I remember having to sit through an interminable JCC Board meeting, where the issue of whether to serve coffee or cocoa at an upcoming ice skating event took fully thirty minutes of discussion. I decided right then that I would not serve another term.

These experiences broadened my perspective, introducing me to interesting people and teaching me something about boards and power. But I wanted more than to be circumscribed by the very few avenues open to women. The local Jewish women's organizations were not satisfying. They filled an empty place in me for a while, but ultimately I wanted to be out there where the action was. In 1963, a year after Rachel was born, Betty Friedan's *The Feminine Mystique* was published, and I read it cover to cover. I remember reading in bed at night and pushing at Bob's arm, saying to him, "How does she know exactly how I feel?" That's where I learned there were more women than I could have imagined with the same sense of yearning to do something and be somebody important. It gave me a lot of confidence to realize that I wasn't alone.

The United Way offered me a solid beginning. Indeed, since the late 1950s, the United Way has been the thread – both volunteer and professional -- that has run almost continuously throughout my life in Worcester. I first became a door-to-door solicitor over fifty years ago, and I am still involved today through the Women's Initiative. My introduction to the organization came through Temple Emanuel: in 1957, my first mentor, Anita Robbins, who was president of Sisterhood, asked me to be part of her United Way team. The United Way's Women's Division included twenty-four women's teams responsible for soliciting street by street in the residential areas of the city and the contiguous towns. (Male volunteers handled all of the commercial solicitations.) There were the junior league team, teams from different parts of the city and surrounding towns, and our team, Residential Team 18, then called "the Jewish team." The term wasn't meant to be derogatory or dismissive; it simply described one of the distinctions among the teams.

Our team's territory encompassed the west side of Worcester. I often packed up my kids and took them in the car with me when I went door to door to ask for donations; I thought people were likely to give me more money that way. Most of the people I solicited were quite responsive. Everybody knew about the United Way, and there really was no other major community campaign at that time. Now, of course, there are organized solicitations for all types of medical research, as well as for a host of other causes. When I started, however, the United Way really stood by itself. I remember when it was still called the Community Chest in the early 1950s, and when the red feather was used as a symbol, both locally and nationally.

Every few weeks during the annual campaign, a breakfast was held for solicitors so that each division could report on its progress. People tooted horns, and everyone cheered when a division head announced a large number of contributions. It was really a wonderful thing to be part of something big that was community-wide.

There was always great competition between the men's and the women's teams. My particular goal was to trounce the men's team that solicited small businesses. The very last day of the campaign was called "Free Day." One was allowed to go anywhere in the community and ask for contributions as long as there had been no previous solicitation. The women would go all over town; we wanted to make 100%. It was ours for the taking.

Everybody knows how single-minded and determined I am, not to mention competitive. One year, I decided to go up to the airport. There weren't a lot of planes flying in and out in those days, either, but several airlines were still based in Worcester. In the terminal, I went to the check-in desks for each airline and asked all of the employees if they had made a contribution to the United Way. They felt bad because there weren't very many people there to solicit. After I finished talking to them, one man waved at another area of the airport and said, "You know, there is a whole group of guys over there. Just drive around, and they may be willing to give you some money."

I climbed into my car and followed their directions. All of a sudden, I looked in my rearview mirror, and there was a cruiser behind me with the lights flashing. He pulled me over, jumped out, and snapped at me, "Where in the hell do you think you're going, lady?"

I pointed and said, "I'm going to go over there and ask for their contribution to the United Way."

He looked at me and said, "You are on the active runway. That's the control tower you're driving to."

And I said, "Oh!" Then I paused. "Have *you* given yet to the United Way?"

He burst out laughing. And I had to turn around. Somehow that story got into the paper the next day, and it was the biggest joke around.

After a few years, I became captain of the Jewish team and then, ultimately, the head of the Women's Division, encompassing all of the 24 residential teams. I ended up knowing every road in Worcester as well as in all of the contiguous towns. Not only did I regularly have to meet with the team captains in each community, but I also often had to follow up on cards that hadn't been done near the end of the campaign. I was especially concerned about collecting the bigger pledges from retired business owners, who often gave us a lot of money. So I drove all around the back roads of Shrewsbury, Leicester, Grafton, West Boylston and Boylston etc. Of course, we always made 100% of the goal for our division.

I believe that women have an instinctive understanding of the nature of stewardship. Every year, when the campaign ended, I sat down and wrote thank you notes to each of the twenty-four team captains, thanking them for their hard work and recognizing individual efforts. No one told me to do that; it was obviously the right thing to do. Today, when I see a large organization failing to acknowledge its donors, I say to myself, you don't need a Ph.D. to learn Stewardship 101. As women volunteers, we knew very well that people volunteer out of the goodness of their hearts. Though they might claim not to require any thanks, everyone needs to be valued.

As my involvement in the community continued, each door that opened led to another, a pattern that has recurred throughout my volunteer and professional careers. To some extent, I owed that phenomenon to a natural mentoring among women. Anita Robbins had brought me first into Sisterhood and then into the United Way. Frances L. Hiatt especially took me under her wing; she was a community advocate whose husband, Jacob, was a renowned philanthropist. Frances drew me onto the Planning Council of the United Way and, later, encouraged me to join the board of the Visiting Nurses Association (VNA). She often called the house, asking the children, "Dahling, is your mother home?" And one of the kids would say, "Just a minute, Mrs. Hiatt." When I picked up the phone, she would say, "Dahling, howevah did they know who it was?" Now, Mrs. Hiatt grew up not far from Bob, on the east side of Worcester, so it was quite amusing to hear her speak. But she was a real mentor to me, very down to earth. She shared her insights and her experience. She made cookies for my children. She was probably one of the most important influences in my life.

In the 1970s, I was a corporator at WCIS, and Frances was a member of the bank's board. One fall, she wasn't feeling well. When I asked her how she was, she said, "I have a malaise. I can't eat, and I don't feel good." She stopped wanting to see anybody. I remember writing her notes. By December, it turned out that she had pancreatic cancer. She died maybe a month or so after her diagnosis. On the day she died, a note I had written to her got to the family. Jack Hiatt asked me to be a pallbearer at her funeral. Never before or since have I heard of a woman's serving as a pallbearer, but that's how close I was to Frances Hiatt.

In conjunction with my work in the United Way campaigns, in the late 1960s I was asked to serve on the board of the Edward Street Day Care Center. Prominent local women who were committed to social service had founded Edward Street in the late 19th century. There were no Jews on its board. But there I was! It was the most amazing experience. I loved Edward Street because the men and women involved were so effective at promoting its mission. During my time there, we hired Dory

Rourke as director. She and I remain colleagues and friends to this day. Edward Street marked my first experience on a non-Jewish community board. As I became first treasurer and then vice-president, I marveled at the respect with which I was treated. I might have become an adult, with children and responsibilities of my own, but the uncertain little girl I had been was still very much with me. With every important position I have ever had, I have asked myself, "how could this possibly be happening to me?" I had been told about my failings too many times when I was a child to expect that I deserved success. Yet, at the same time, I knew I was too capable to relegate myself to the tedious day-to-day duties of the fifties housewife. That dichotomy remains with me, a curious blend of supreme confidence and astonishment that anyone else could believe that I was talented or had the slightest thing to contribute.

In the late 1950's, I was asked to be part of the formation of the Women's Division of the Worcester Jewish Federation. The woman who came to talk to us at our initial meeting was none other than Adeline Bishop, my mother, whose experience in the Hartford Jewish Federation made her a valuable advisor to other start-up women's divisions. I served as a campaign chairman and then as president of the Women's Division. While I was campaign chairman, I was invited to attend a meeting of the General Assembly of the Council of Jewish Federations and Welfare Funds (CJF) to give a presentation to their Women's Communal Service Committee on how we had solicited women in country clubs. I stayed at the fancy Diplomat Hotel in Hollywood, Florida. I was very nervous about my talk. I had worked hard on it; this would be my first opportunity to speak publicly in a national forum. The day I was to speak, the weather was gorgeous. When I walked into the conference room, there were only two people there: the director of the Women's Communal Service Committee and a friend of my mother's! Everyone else was at the beach.

But this speaking opportunity propelled me onto the national stage of Jewish philanthropy and organizations. Soon after, I was asked to serve on the Women's Communal Services Committee. At another General Assembly held in St. Louis a few years later, I was invited to attend a two-day workshop for women, held prior to the full General Assembly, to learn how to train other women to become better solicitors. At the close of the conference, I attended a banquet with 2000 other people, where we listened to a speaker whose words changed my entire approach to community service. The room was very large and very crowded, and the man lectured from a distant podium. Slight and soft-spoken, he looked like a specter, almost an apparition. His name was Elie Wiesel, speaking publicly for the very first time about his experiences as a Holocaust survivor. You could have heard a pin drop when he said, " Had we known in that kingdom of night that you *knew* and did nothing, we would have all died of despair."

I left that room realizing that to remain silent and stand idly by while others were in trouble or suffering was not tolerable. I made a promise to myself never to be guilty of that. It hasn't always been easy to stand up and be counted or go against public opinion, but I have learned that each individual voice can indeed make a difference and change the outcome.

In 1971, I was asked to go on a ten-day trip for the CJF in order to advise and consult with the Jewish communities in Marseilles, Copenhagen, and Rome. There were twelve of us in the group, including one other woman. The CJF categorized cities into small, intermediate and large. In our group, we were all from intermediate-sized cities. For this particular mission, they didn't want to send a contingent from large cities, where people were usually involved only in the work of a single community board. To the other extreme, small communities didn't have many Jewish institutions at all. But in intermediate locales, like Worcester, there were typically synagogues, a federation, a Jewish Community Center, Jewish Family Service and a home for the aged. Over time, most community volunteers sat on the boards of most of them.

In Europe, we were treated like kings and queens, invited into homes, wined and dined. They greeted us as though we were a delegation sent from heaven to rescue them. It was twenty-five years after the war, but many of their young people had left, immigrating especially to Israel, and they were trying desperately to hang onto their communities.

After this unbelievable trip, I traveled home in the middle of the night, flying from Kennedy to Boston and arriving at two in the morning instead of 10 p.m. as anticipated. Bob, who had been alone with the children for ten days, met me at the airport, shaking his finger at me. "If you ever pull this shit on me again," he warned, "there won't be anyone there to meet you."

He was joking, of course. He may have been fed up after dealing with the day-to-day demands of being on call for the children, dropping off forgotten Temple books in the middle of the day and dealing with who knows how many sibling skirmishes, but there was no question that he supported everything I did.

This was about the time I began to hear the rumor that our marriage had to be on shaky ground. What woman would go off and leave her husband like that?

Two years later, in 1973, I was asked to chair the Women's Communal Service Committee of the CJF. At that point, I had been slated to become president of the Edward Street board, but I stepped down to take on this new position. I didn't believe I could do justice to Edward Street in company with these new duties. In 1974, I became the Secretary of the CJF Board. When I was newly elected, they were having new stationary printed, and a woman called to tell me I was going to be listed as "Mrs. Robert F. Green." I told her my name was Lois Green. She said I would be the only woman listed that way. I said, "Well, that's still my name."

She called me again and told me I was now going to be listed as "Mrs. Lois Green."

"Are the men listed as 'Mr.'?"

"No."

"Well," I said. "I just wanted to be listed as Lois B. Green."

"But then no one will know you are married."

"I didn't think I was elected to the board or as secretary in order to let people know I was married," I retorted. "I thought it didn't matter."

I traveled all over the country for the CJF, talking about voluntarism and offering workshops on solicitation techniques. I went to Milwaukee, Los Angeles, Dallas, New Orleans, among many other places. Before my tenure ended, I believe I attended twenty General Assemblies. Moreover, from 1970 to 1975, I also belonged to the National Council of the American Jewish Joint Distribution Committee (JDC) and served as a member of the National Women's Division for the United Jewish Appeal.

My involvement with the United Way in Worcester continued to develop during this period. Beginning in 1973, I served on the Board of Directors three different times, a commitment that would last well over three decades and bring with it a number of different positions and committee appointments. Early on, I was named to the Finance Committee. There were five of us, including an accountant and a president of a company, among others. I spent some time trying to figure out what I was supposed to know. And then one day at our noon meeting, I said, "I don't quite understand this. How did the comptroller get from here to here?" The comptroller explained it and asked, "Is that helpful?" I said, "Not really." He repeated it, and I said, "I'll tell you what. It's only an hour's meeting, and I don't want to keep everybody else who already understands this. I will stay afterwards while he walks me through it."

The other four men said, "No, I think maybe we ought to figure this one out." I ended up being right. The comptroller had done something unclear. Nobody got angry with me, including the comptroller. I was right, but I hadn't made them wrong. I was always outspoken, but I learned how to deal with my own outspokenness. I never confronted. I never said, "What you're doing is wrong." When I first became involved in the community, I used to think that everybody would think I was one of those stereotyped Jews and aggressive females. Yet no matter how much I opened my big mouth, people respected me, and each step brought me to another step. In part, I believe that my success came because I learned at the very beginning not to be a woman who wanted to be a man. Instead, I wanted to be the woman who brought the skills that I knew a woman had to the boardroom.

Now matter how active I had become in volunteer organizations, both local and national, I was still searching for something else. As part of that search, I repeatedly took evening classes at Clark University in the 1960s and early 1970s. In 1965, for a seminar in psychology, I wrote a final paper about why mothers should be allowed to stay with their children who were in the hospital overnight. Later, that paper became instrumental in changing the rules about parental visitation in the Worcester hospitals. I also took a class in Cultural Anthropology, taught by a professor named Sanford Gerber. I was the only older person in a class of young students. Gerber was full of generalizations, and from the very beginning, he and I tended to clash. When he commented that all French airline pilots drank, for example, I would raise my hand and say, "You can't stereotype all French airline pilots. That's ridiculous."

Near the end of the semester, in December, he announced that he had been born Jewish but never practiced. He claimed that no one would identify him as a Jew.

Up went my hand. "Dr. Gerber," I said. "I immediately defined you as Jewish, and I'm sure that everybody who meets you defines you as Jewish. You're probably the only one who doesn't."

He was aghast. At the next class, right before the winter holidays, I gave him a book called *The Island Within*, a memoir about a young man's search for Judaism. When we returned to class in January, he pointed his finger at me and said, "You did quite a job on me." That book had thrown him for a loop.

Then, in 1973, Clark was working to create a program in Jewish Studies at the university, financed in part by the Worcester Jewish Federation. I heard through the grapevine that Saul Cohen, the graduate dean, was going to name Sanford Gerber as head of the program. I said to myself, "This cannot possibly be my Sanford Gerber."

But it was. I had heard that he had not only found his Jewish identity but also had become Orthodox and a big champion of Jewish causes. I called up the Dean and told him I wanted to come in to see him. He knew who I was; by then, I was a known quantity. I told him that it made me quite uneasy that someone with no Jewish background or history of Jewish identification was going to take over the program now that he had suddenly become very observant.

"It is not my business to tell you how to run the college," I said, "but if you do appoint him, I will march outside with a placard."

I don't know exactly what happened, but Sanford Gerber never became the head of Jewish Studies at Clark.

In 1968, I read *The Women's Room* by Marilyn French. I sat on the couch with the book in my lap one long Sunday and read all day. Around dinnertime, Bob and the kids came in to see what and when we were going to eat. "If you want dinner," I snapped, "fix it yourself!"

I was transfixed. Just as had Friedan's *Feminine Mystique*, French's description of women in the fifties, trapped by social mores and gender roles, showed me unequivocally that I was not the only woman of my generation who felt as though their natural talents had been wasted. The characters' push to cut loose from domestic servitude galvanized me. No wonder I still found myself at loose ends.

CHAPTER FOUR

BALANCING FAMILY AND CAREER

"Children will not remember you for the material things you provided but for the feeling that you cherished them."

-Richard L. Evans

I don't think I ever fit the mold of the traditional fifties housewife and mother. Instead, I tried to balance the needs of my family with my own need to be out doing something -- in the Temple, the community and the world beyond the narrow confines of my neighborhood. When the children went to Lee Street School, I made sure that I was home at noon because they came home for lunch every day. I was also there every afternoon at three o'clock, so I could hear how the day had gone. In fact, I can remember quite a few times when I raced to be home on time, and nobody showed up.

They were all playing at their friends' houses.

But there were also times when I had to call one of the neighbors to watch them because I was running late because of a meeting. I often had meetings in the late afternoon, after the children were home from school for the day. I would get everything ready for dinner and say to Rachel, "At four o'clock, take the chicken out of the refrigerator, turn the oven on to 350 degrees and I will be home by five or five-thirty." One day, she said, "How come you always ask me to do it even though I'm the youngest? You never ask Sarah, David or Patty." And I said, "Because I know you'll do it. Otherwise, I would have to call and remind them. This way, I don't even have to think about it." She couldn't have been more than nine or ten years old, but she said, "You know, Mom, you're going to make me more responsible and them less responsible."

I do expect that my children occasionally felt that I wasn't paying enough attention to them. From the time they were small and I became involved in the United Way and the Jewish Federation, my activities multiplied exponentially. I was often at a meeting, and I spent a lot of time on the telephone. I'm sure it was hard when I went away, traveling for the Council of Jewish Federation and Welfare Funds, though I never was gone for more than a day or two. My oldest used to take my sweater to bed with her until I returned. In fact, Sarah said to me one day, "I wish I were a Jew in Romania because you worry more about the Jews in Romania than you do about me."

When I spoke around the country, I often came home exhausted, especially if I had been gone for just a day, speaking early and returning that same night. Doing a training or delivering a speech is like being on stage, driven by adrenalin.

Most of the time, it went very well, and I would drive home from the airport elated, anxious to tell everyone about the brilliant job I had done. But as I opened the back door, one of the children would call, "Mommy! David won't let me ...." or "Mommy! What's for dinner?" In two seconds, I was back on Rutland Terrace, a regular mommy and housewife. My great successes remained out there somewhere, where only I could relish them. I think Bob always asked me how it had gone. But when I walked in the house, every complaint in the world came rushing at me. Mine were no different from other children. They grounded me.

If my children had a problem, if somebody hurt their feelings, I was always there. I don't think they ever complained that I wasn't at home all the time like everyone else's mothers. But I learned to take my cues from them. One afternoon, I was standing at the sink, and one of my daughters came home from school and wanted to talk to me. All of a sudden, she took my face in her two hands, turned it to her and said, "I'm telling you something. Look at me." From that point on, if any of them needed to talk, I sat down at the kitchen table so they would feel that they had my full attention.

Of course, they always made fun of me, even while they were growing up. They all still tease me about being bossy, or bragging, or talking about myself. For some reason, David started calling me "Lois" when he was about 12. I never chastised him, because it was said in such a loving way. He wasn't being fresh. He had Bob's sense of humor, too, so even when he was bad I used to laugh. He'd say, "Oh, come on, Lois," and instead of being angry with him I would laugh. Or if I picked at him, he would call me "Sophie," for Mrs. Portnoy in *Portnoy's Complaint*. The dangers of having a child who reads! My children made it absolutely impossible for me to take myself too seriously.

Bob played a large role in providing consistency in our family life. Very early in our marriage, right after Sarah was born, he had said to me, "You know, I probably won't make a lot of money because I'm not going out at night to sell life insurance. I'm going to be home every night for dinner." And he was. In fact, I never could have taken on outside responsibilities without Bob's support. He was always there. He chipped in with the laundry, the dishes, getting supper ready. He took turns with me getting up at night when the children were babies. If my babysitter didn't show up and I had to be at an important meeting, Bob would leave the office and come home so I could go. Perhaps it was because his mother had worked; he knew how to do everything necessary to keep a household going. But somehow, from the time we met and he so easily became a part of the Bryn Mawr world I loved, he always understood not only who I was but also what I wanted and needed to be.

Just like the children, he grounded me. When I took evening classes at Clark, for example, he was home to feed the children. I felt guilty being out at dinnertime twice a week, so on Tuesdays I would make a brisket with onions, potatoes and carrots. It was a complete meal that they could then eat cold on Thursday night.

One night, I came in the back door and Bob was standing there.

"There has been a revolution in this house," he told me.

"What happened?" I asked, alarmed.

He said, "The kids said if you serve one more piece of brisket, they will throw it at you when you get home."

"But what will you do if I don't cook?"

"I'll cook," he said. "Or we'll go out, or have pizza."

Not many husbands at that time would have responded that way. I wish I could make young people today understand how far from the norm he was. I watch today as my son and my sons-in-law share childcare and cooking with their wives. I do know that there are many things that still need to be changed. But in my generation, it was an indisputable fact that married women stayed at home. That was your job. You made the dinner, you took care of the children, you did the laundry and the ironing, you changed the sheets. If you wanted to volunteer, that was fine, as long as it didn't interfere with your duties as a housewife. I had an allowance! I didn't have any money of my own. I loved to go antiquing with my friends, Barbara Greenberg and Joan Sadowsky, and so I would save from my allowance until I had enough to buy a little something. That was the beginning of my collecting Chinese export celadon porcelain. (Years later, after Bob died, I sold most of it and created the Robert F. and Lois B. Green Fund at the Greater Worcester Community Foundation.) Sometimes I borrowed money from Barbara or Joan. I never wanted to ask Bob. In fact, I remember once he got angry with me for spending $25 on a hat for a Sisterhood event. It was a totally different environment. And yet Bob was most unusual in his involvement not only with the children but also with our household in general.

I may not have followed a strictly traditional path, yet my children were – and are – such an essential part of my life that it would be a mistake to emphasize only the time I spent away from them. We were a very close family. We played games together; we had Shabbat dinner as a family; we enjoyed being together. We went apple picking every fall, we went to the penny candy store. One of our rituals was the family meeting. If we were trying to decide what to do that day or which restaurant to go to, Bob would say, "Okay! Family meeting time!" Everybody would groan, including me, but then everyone had an equal voice. The majority ruled. Shabbat dinner brought another family ritual. It was the only night the children were required to be at home for dinner. Every Friday night, like clockwork, Bob would ask, "What was the most outstanding thing that happened to you this week?" It could be bad or good, but everyone had to go around the table and answer in turn. Even though they complained, it was a tradition, and secretly the children were pleased with it. When their friends came for dinner, I would hear them whisper, "My father's going to ask you about the most outstanding thing that happened to you this week. You just have to bear with it and do it."

As they grew older, my two youngest, Patty and Rachel, went on field trips with me. We often went to Filene's in Natick, way back when they had a lunchroom, to shop and have lunch. Patty also loved to jump into the car with me and do errands. She's forty-nine years old now, and she still loves for us to run errands together.

Like most of us, I get a kick out of looking back at some of our interactions, especially when the children were teenagers. At some point in the mid-1960s, I remember reading Haim Ginott's book on parenting, *Between Parent and Child*. As an example of positive parenting, Dr. Ginnott advised that when your child gets off the bus and the bus driver is angry at him or her, let the bus driver's mother worry about the bus driver, and you worry about your own child. You were supposed to say, "That must have been hard for you when he yelled at you," taking the child's side instead of immediately assuming it was his or her fault.

So one day, David came up the stairs and left his shoes in the hall. I almost tripped over them. I had just been reading Ginott's book, and I thought, what a great parenting tool! Instead of yelling and bossing, I would try this approach. When you yell a lot, they don't pay any attention anyway; they just roll their eyes in their heads. By this point, David was in his room, lying on his bed. I said, "David, could you pick up your shoes? I'm afraid someone will trip."

"Okay, Mom," he said.

I went into my room, and the shoes were still there when I came out. On my way downstairs, I said in my most reasonable tone of voice, "David, please pick up your shoes."

The next time I came up, there the shoes were. So this time I said, "David, you know it makes me quite unhappy when you leave your shoes in the way." I quoted Dr. Ginott exactly. I went into my bedroom for something, came out again, and they were still there!

So I yelled. "You know what?" I shrieked. "You're not only deaf, you're dumb, too! Get the heck out of your bed and pick up your shoes!"

He did.

And I put away Dr. Ginott.

That whole theory was so foreign to my personality; it never worked. I remember saying to one of my children who wanted advice, "But what do you think?" And she said, "I wouldn't

have asked you if I didn't want your opinion!" I did learn not
to offer too honest an opinion about clothing choices. If one of
the girls asked me to tell her which dress she should wear and I
said, "wear that one," she would say, "what do you mean? You
don't like the other one?" After awhile, I began to ask, "Well,
which one do you think you'd like to wear tonight?" Early on, I
figured out how to handle the issue of curfews. I would ask the
children what time they thought it was reasonable to be home.
Inevitably, they picked a time much earlier than I might have
suggested. Once, I remember, Patty was angry with me because
I had refused to let her go to the movies. Bob and I came home
to find that she had defaced the photograph of me with Golda
Meir, one of my prize possessions. Patty had colored Golda's
nose with Magic Marker and then, feeling terribly guilty, tried
to scratch it off. I am certain that I am the only person in the
world who has a picture of Golda Meir with a missing nose!

Just as the beach had been an important part of my own
childhood, it defined our family life when my children were
growing up. Every summer, we spent two and a half months
at the same cottage in Woodmont, where I had grown up. My
mother had inherited it from my grandmother and in turn had
given it to me. Until 1971, when we sold it, we left Worcester
right after school ended in June and didn't come home until
after Labor Day. All of my friends' children went off to camp
for the summers, and the mothers played golf and did whatever
they wanted. I didn't want my kids to go away. Sarah did
go twice, for a few weeks, but none of the others wanted to
leave. We were together for the entire summer. There were no
meetings, ballet classes or orthodontist appointments. At the
beach, I never went out with friends during the week. I was

just with my children. Once in awhile, when Bob came down on weekends, we might go out for dinner on a Saturday night. But he was content to be at home with the family, and so was I. I had a different kind of relationship with my children at the beach. We shared everything. There is no question in my mind that my spending those summers with them had a deep impact on all of us.

We had such a good time together. The pattern of our days at the beach mimicked my childhood experience. We went to the movies on rainy days and out for dinner sometimes during the week and, of course, spent a lot of time in the water and on the beach. All of the children in the neighborhood came to our house to play ball in our side yard or sit on the seawall and look out at the ocean. Years before, my mother had had a friend who was a doctor at Yale. He had told her that one shouldn't ever sit in the sun between the hours of 12 and 2 p.m. So, when I was a child, our routine was to go the beach in the morning, come up for lunch between 12 and 2 and then go back in mid-afternoon. During the off hours, we ate lunch and played games. I repeated this same schedule with my own family.

We loved to do puzzles together. We played Monopoly and Go-Fish and War. My children grew up to play those same games with their own children. Now, when we get together, I also play Yahtzee and cribbage with my grandchildren, and I can guarantee that they, too, will teach those games to their children. It's all about building traditions.

Of course, my competitive edge didn't disappear just because I happened to be playing with my children. I remember playing backgammon with Rachel when she was about 10 or 11. If she was really beating me, I would hit the bridge table with my elbows and all of the pieces would go flying. She'd scream at me, "Mommies are supposed to let their kids win!" And I would scream back, "Not this Mommy!" Bob would come in from the other room and say, "I cannot believe that the two of you are in here yelling at each other!"

At some point, I got sick and tired of sweeping up all of the sand the children constantly tracked in from the beach. There I was, twice a day morning and night, yelling at them because they weren't hosing off well enough. One day, it occurred to me that I had begun to sound like my mother, always shouting and criticizing. We had such wonderful summers together that I was afraid I was spoiling it for the children by nagging them all the time.

I said to them, "You know, I'm tired of bugging you. You roll your eyes in your head about my picking on you, and I'm not going to do that anymore."

I made a deal with them. If they helped me clean the house every Thursday – and by cleaning, I meant bathrooms, the kitchen floor and everything – I promised not to nag them the rest of the week. That way the house would be clean before Bob arrived for the weekend. He was Mr. Clean himself; you could do open heart surgery on his desk. Being married to me must have been incredibly difficult for him.

All four of them agreed. I had to grit my teeth all week as I tried to ignore the sand all over the house. On Thursdays, they really pitched in. We vacuumed the furniture and the floors. They were wonderful. And I learned something. We were at the beach, for God's sake! Of course there was sand! Cleaning together actually gave us even more time together. Now I didn't have to be in the house washing and doing floors and bathrooms while they were outside playing.

On Thursday nights, after the cleaning, we went out for supper. We couldn't go to a "Daddy's restaurant," which we defined as expensive, but we could go to one that was nicer than usual. Every Thursday night, they got to choose. We might go to a little fish place or to Lender's Bagels, for lox and cream cheese.

By the time we finally sold the cottage in 1971, the neighborhood had deteriorated. There were motorcycle gangs, and I couldn't let the children go out at night. Bob used to say he would drive down on Friday nights and hope that we were still there. So I bit the bullet and put the place on the market. The day we signed the papers in the lawyer's office, I began to shake with chills. I thought I was coming down with the flu. When we left, I said to Bob, "You'd better get me home. I'm sick." Within an hour, I was fine. It must have been the trauma of selling the place I loved most. I had spent almost forty years of my life there.

The following summer, in 1972, we went on a big cross-country trip. Two other families in the neighborhood were going, too, and we were all leaving on the same day. The night before we left, we had a potluck dinner; we planned to have another potluck dinner when we all came home so we could compare notes. Everybody was going to visit the national parks. One family was getting in the car and traveling without plans, intending to stop at random along the way. The second family had made reservations to stay in the parks and planned to visit friends as they drove west. My family had reservations for every single night. I had spent six months figuring out exactly how many miles it was between the Grand Canyon and Zion, what time we would leave, how long it would take to get there etc. That's how I booked our reservations, all along the way.

We were gone for three weeks, the longest time Bob had ever taken off from work. Sarah stayed home; she had finished her freshman year of college and didn't want to come with us. I felt bad because it was a fabulous trip. When we came home, we visited with the neighbors and everyone else had had a good time, too. Even though we went to many of the same places, we never ran into one another. It was a wonderful experience.

The following summer, we stayed home, and everyone hated it. Sarah waitressed, and David worked in our friend's factory, making handbags. All of the kids protested at the end of the summer. And so, in 1973, Bob and I went to visit the Cape, Rhode Island and the North Shore, looking for a new beach to adopt. We settled on Gloucester, where we knew people. We put the children in the car and drove around with a real estate agent, looking at rental properties. Finally, she pulled up to an old brown house, far out on a promontory, the ocean surrounding it. She went off to get the keys, and the moment she returned, the children and I said, "We'll take it." I thought Bob was going to shoot us. He had told us we were supposed to negotiate, but we had already lost our hearts. The cottage, called Brown Boulder, was 100 years old and filled with nooks and crannies. It was the perfect house for us.

We spent two fabulous summers there. The house was right next to Good Harbor Beach. We'd go down to the beach in the morning, come up for a few hours at noon and then go back at three. On rainy days, we played games, went to the movies and visited the Peabody Museum in Salem. We were together just the way we had been in Connecticut. I remember once saying to David, "You know, it's time for you to do something in the summer." He said, "But Mom, I have a job!"

"And what's your job?" I asked.

"I watch out for tidal waves and water spouts. Have you seen any?"

During our second summer in Gloucester, in 1975, I was diagnosed with uterine cancer, and our family life shifted on its foundation. It was the first time my children had realized that a parent might die. We all were afraid I might die. Sarah had just graduated college and had left to seek her fortune in Los Angeles, David was in college, but Patty was 14, just starting at Doherty High School, and Rachel was only 12. There had been hard times before, of course, but this was the biggest challenge we had faced so far. And we faced it as a family.

CHAPTER FIVE

MOVING FORWARD

*"Life is what happens to you
while you are busy making other plans."*

-John Lennon

One evening in late July 1975, during our second summer in Gloucester, we were all having pizza with our oldest, dearest friends, the Ashers, and their kids. I wasn't feeling well, and I went up to the bathroom, where I discovered that I was hemorrhaging. There were two bathrooms, side by side, and my friend, Lenny Asher, said to me, "Lois, are you all right?" I said, "No. I think you'd better go home." So they left, and I came downstairs and told Bob, "I think I need to get to a hospital."

I called my gynecologist in Worcester, who suggested that I go to the hospital in Gloucester. But I wanted to drive back home so I could go to Memorial Hospital. It was only an hour and a half away, and the children could follow in my car. Bob lay me down with a lot of towels in the backseat of his gorgeous new

Mercedes. Afterwards, I always said that was the moment when I realized just how much he loved me! We arrived at Memorial about eleven that night, and when they came to take me out of the car, I said, "You don't understand. If you lift me out of here and sit me up, it will be a disaster." Of course, nobody believed me. They sat me up, and whoosh, I hemorrhaged again. At that point, they took me into the emergency room – flat on a gurney, this time – and the resident leaned over me. He had an accent, and I asked him where he was from. When he told me he had grown up in "Persia" rather than Iran, I asked, "are you Jewish?" "Yes," he answered. "Well," I said, sitting straight up again, "have I got a girl for you!" I think he already had a girlfriend. Later, I invited them both for Rosh Hashanah.

The doctors couldn't stop the bleeding, so about midnight I went up to the operating room for a D and C. The next morning, I was allowed to get up and go to the bathroom, but I passed out because I had lost so much blood. I split my cheek open. Late in the afternoon, they sent me to see a cosmetic surgeon, but not before they sent a risk management team in to question me about the fainting spell. They were afraid I was going to sue them.

"Does this happen to you often?" they asked.

"Only when I've lost this much blood," I retorted.

The next day, I was allowed to go back to Gloucester while we waited for the results from the biopsy they had taken during the D and C. Almost immediately, however, I had to turn around and return to Worcester because they had discovered a tumor in the lining of the uterus. They had to do a hysterectomy. My mother came from Hartford to stay with the children. I had the surgery and, at the end of the week, I sent Bob back to the beach for the weekend. He planned to come back home with the children on Sunday.

That Friday night about seven o'clock, I looked up to see my gynecologist at the door of my hospital room. And I knew. Doctors just don't visit patients at that time in the evening. He told me the tumor was malignant. He drew me a picture of where it was located and promised to return the next morning so we could talk some more. It was a lot for me to absorb all at once, and I was alone. I called Bob in Gloucester, told him the news and asked him to pack up the kids and come home. My mother and sister, who were with my family, made plans to come to Worcester the next day, as did my stepfather in Hartford. At that point, I fell back on my usual coping mechanism: I couldn't keep my eyes open. The nurses came in to give me a back rub, which is what they used to do for patients at bedtime in those days. I told them I was too tired and rolled over and went to sleep. About four in the morning, I woke up, and the whole world crashed.

That day, however, I realized that I couldn't fall apart because everyone else already had. My mother was hysterical, my sister was crying. My stepfather was a basket case. I am the biggest coward in the world. I hate pain. But this time, I had to be the strong one, trying to calm everyone down. It was like an out-of-body experience, watching myself as the star in this performance. I was strong and reassuring. I told them everything was going to be all right and that they needed to be strong for the children. I tried to hold everyone together.

After I came home, I remember being in my bedroom, and all the children were sitting around me on the bed. Sarah, who had moved to California earlier that summer, had come home that week when she found out I was sick. Patty was just going into high school. That afternoon, she asked, "But who's going to help me buy my new clothes for school?" The others got angry with her. I told them, "Don't be angry with her. Everybody reflects on something that happens in terms of how it's going to matter in their lives." And I said to Patty, "Either Joan or Barbara will take you," referring to my two friends whom she loved. And she said, "Okay." That's what she needed to know.

They did six weeks of radiation, and the thirty-five treatments exhausted me. I would come home and climb into bed. It was tough going. But the kids were wonderful. David took me for treatment several times before he went to college in the fall, so that he could see what it was like for me. Patty would come home from school and check to make sure I was all right and then go off. But Rachel would come into the house every day after school and want to know how I was and if I'd eaten lunch. She would bring her homework and do it in the bedroom with me. Everyone who called to check on me asked for Rachel, because she was the one who was most aware of the details.

People were very kind. They brought food, and they called. But there were others who couldn't talk to me. Nobody actually said the word "cancer." It was "the Big C" then. And I was only 45 years old. I remember going to the doctor's office for a check up, and somebody I knew very well looked up from her magazine and saw me. I watched her head go back down as she pretended she hadn't noticed me. At the time, the doctor had said I had an 85% chance of survival. Bob's reaction was that I was completely cured. But I said, "Well, somebody turns out to be in that 15%." The most difficult part of the whole cancer experience is that no one else wants to talk about the realities of what you're facing. It's just too hard for them.

During radiation treatment, I had a lot of trouble eating, and I lost about thirty pounds. Given my issues with weight, I was delighted with the way I looked. I thought I was beautiful. Then one afternoon, Patty hugged me and pulled away. "I don't want to hug you anymore," she said. "You're all bones." I realized then what I must look like to other people.

Not long after, Bob asked me, "If you could have anything you wanted to eat, what would it be?"

I thought for a minute, and then I said, "I would like baked custard."

"Do you think you can get downstairs?"

"I think so," I answered.

He sat me at the kitchen table, opened the *Joy of Cooking* to the custard recipe and put it down in front of me. Then, as we discussed it step by step, he made baked custard for me.

When I had finished radiation, I decided that I had two choices. I could sit around and wait to die. Or I could get on with my life. I began to consider the idea of going back to school. I had always wanted to pursue a master's in social work, not to work in direct care but to become an administrator. But I decided that it would be too difficult for the family. There were no social work programs in Worcester, and I would have had to travel to Boston. As I have always said, when one door closes, another one opens. In the mail arrived an announcement from Clark University about a new master's program in public administration. That's it, I said to myself. That's what I want to do. The program was really for people who were already working in the field, but I asked someone I knew from the United Way to write a letter of recommendation for me. I was accepted, and so I went back to school.

I was forty-five years old, and I hadn't been in school for 24 years. I tried to convince myself that it was all right if I didn't get all A's in all of my classes, but I never did believe it. I worked incredibly hard, turning my life around so that I woke up early to do my homework before the children got up. In the end, the only course I didn't get an A in was Statistics, where I received a B+. Who in the world could remember that two minuses equaled a plus? At any rate, I learned a lot about myself during my two years in graduate school. Although I wasn't particularly good at remembering dates and how to do footnotes, I was much more knowledgeable than the other students because of my experiences. I did well on my essays. Bob and the kids were wonderfully supportive. I wrote my final thesis on advisory committees that were without the authority or power to put their suggestions into effect. I used my own experience as a member of the Office for Human Services Advisory Committee in Worcester, to which I had been appointed by the city manager. After I graduated in the spring of 1978, I contemplated going on for a Ph.D., but after I had continued my community work for a year or so, a friend who had been in the program with me said, "Enough stalling around! Go out there and get a real job."

In 1980, I took a job in Shrewsbury at the Irving Glavin Regional Center, a residential center under the aegis of the Massachusetts Department of Mental Retardation. Opened in 1975, Glavin grew out of new approaches to caring for the developmentally disabled that emerged in the 1960s and 1970s.

My first job at Glavin was to do training for the Central

Massachusetts region. The second year I was there, they moved me to the evaluation team. There were three of us. We were called out to investigate whenever there was a concern about abuse of clients or patients in a hospital or residential care setting. Sometimes I went to community residences, or I met with actual program leaders to investigate an allegation. I remember the first time I went to Worcester State Hospital, where we had been asked to follow up on an incident. I was scared. There were all these people lying on the lobby floor or sitting there smoking cigarettes, and I had to step over them to get to the elevator. When I reached my assigned floor, I had to ring a bell before they could let me in and lock the door behind me. It was the first time I had had such an experience.

I learned to interview effectively, finding that I was able to glean a lot of information by asking questions of alleged perpetrators in a very non-threatening way. Sometimes, there was no question in my mind that the patient or client involved was incredibly difficult and had caused the incident. In other cases, I discovered that the problem stemmed from the attitude of an overbearing worker. Often, wonderful people take these jobs, caring with kindness and skill for clients who face significant challenges. Yet a bad apple occasionally slips in. Poor caretakers might feel an inflated sense of power because they have never before had it in their own lives. Their impulse is to take advantage of someone with mental challenges who cannot fight back or defend themselves. It makes for a terrible situation.

In July 1980, the state budget was not finished on time, and all state employees went out on strike. Those of us at Glavin who were not in the union were asked if we would help out.

The center was filled with severely challenged children and adults, and there weren't enough people to take care of them. I had never done direct service, but I had become very attached to some of the Glavin clients. I agreed to come in to help.

To prevent violence, they had told us to come in the middle of the night because there were fewer picketers then. I set my alarm for three a.m. – Bob said he was so proud of me – got myself dressed and drove to the Shrewsbury police station. Two police officers put me in a squad car and drove me to Glavin. As we came down the driveway, we passed strikers holding signs and shaking their fists, yelling "scab!" I was scared to death.

Once we were in the building, they told us to lie down on the floor to see if we could sleep a little longer. No one slept. At five a.m., when they roused us to start the day, they told us they needed help bathing the women and girls. I said, "I can't do that. I don't have any experience. I agreed to come in because I thought I would answer phones or help out in the kitchen." They said, "No, we have the National Guard here for that kind of thing. We need someone to do direct care."

Margaret Foran, a wonderful young woman whom I had met at Glavin, said, "Lois, we can do this together." So we went upstairs and helped one of the residents into the bathtub, using a Hoya lift. After we finished bathing her, the two of us couldn't lift her out, even with the lift.

There was a knock on the door, and a National Guardsman came in, asking if he could help.

I said, "I don't really think that's appropriate."

And he said quietly, "I took this duty because that is my daughter."

He came in and helped us lift her, and we dressed her.

That night, we were about to give the residents peanut butter and crackers as a snack when a staff member walked in and stopped us. "Don't give them peanut butter," she said. "They could easily choke on it and die."

At that point, I was upset that the strike had left the clients at such risk, in charge of volunteers who didn't know how to care for them correctly and could have hurt them, albeit unintentionally. The strike lasted for two days, and we remained at the center for the duration. I think in my whole life I am proudest of those few days. I learned more about myself than at any other time. When I had to do something, I could do it. That same inner strength reappeared when I was taking care of Bob at the end of his life, doing things I would never have believed I could have done.

After the strike at Glavin, Margaret Foran and I became dear friends and saw a lot of each other. I decided that she and my friend, Jim Collins, Vice President of Finance at Clark, and whom I knew also from the VNA finance committee, would be an ideal match. That fall, when I ran into Jim at a reception at Clark, I described Margaret to him as a 15 on a scale of 1 to 10. Margaret was dating someone else at the time, and all year long Jim kept asking me when he could meet this wonderful woman. Finally, in May, I left Margaret a note on her desk telling her that I was planning to leave Glavin to go to Elder Home Care. She left me a return note, saying she wanted to go out for lunch with me before I left, and, by the way, was that man still available? I called Jim immediately, gave him her phone number, and told him he had to call her that very moment because she was sitting at her desk. Not only did they go out for dinner, but they eventually married.

Again, when one door closed, another had opened. As I approached the end of my second year at Glavin, the state found itself in financial trouble and eliminated my position. However, at the same time I had just been asked to serve on the board of Elder Home Care Services, now Elder Services of Worcester. By then, I had already been involved in efforts to support the needs of older people for quite a few years. I had served on the Jewish Healthcare Center Board, the City of Worcester's Commission on Elder Affairs and the Age Center Board. I knew many people in the aging care network, including Sol Boskind, who was then the Executive Director of Elder Home Care.

As a result of my strong volunteer connection to the needs of older adults, I was very happy to join the board of Elder Home Care in the spring of 1982. At the board's annual meeting that May, where I was officially elected, I sat next to Ed McCarthy on the staff at Elder Home Care, whom I had known when he worked at United Way. He told me there was an opening for the position of assistant director. I already knew about the position; a friend who was applying for it had told me about it. I had no intention of jeopardizing my friend's chances by going after the job myself.

The next morning, however, Sol Boskind called me at Glavin and asked me to come in to see him at Elder Home Care. During our meeting, he, too, suggested that I consider applying for the assistant directorship. When I explained that I did not want to compete with the candidate I knew, he told me they had already decided not to hire him because of his youth. Instead, the board had asked Sol to appoint someone who was skilled and mature enough to be able to move up to the position of Executive Director when he retired. I told him that, in that case, I would be very interested. I was about to lose my job at Glavin, and this sounded like a wonderful opportunity.

When the personnel committee, chaired by then Father (later Bishop) George Rueger, interviewed me, they expressed concern that my standards were too high. They were afraid that it would be difficult for me to work with people who didn't meet my expectations. I remember saying that it probably would be difficult, but that I thought I could handle it. Before I was hired, however, I let Sol know that I would have to maintain my commitment to building Bet Shalom, which would take some of my time.

For several years, Sol had chaired the Worcester Jewish Federation's Committee on Older Adults (or COAS), on which I served. COAS drafted a report that called for the need to develop low cost housing for older people in Worcester. In 1977, I became president of the housing board created to build Bet Shalom, or House of Peace, which would provide 70 units of housing for the elderly.

As Sol and I discussed the terms of my new position at Elder Home Care, I asked him for permission to go to the Bet Shalom building site every Thursday morning to attend the construction meetings, run by Haskell Gordon. Even though Haskell was an absolutely wonderful human being and perfectly competent as chair of the building committee, I was such a Boss Murphy that I couldn't miss an on-site meeting, in the trailer, every week. Sol said to me, "What you are doing has to do with the elderly, so it's really part of your job." He gave me blanket permission to leave work whenever I had to go to the City Council or the Planning Board or the Zoning Board on behalf of Bet Shalom. I was so grateful for his support.

Bet Shalom took five years to build, a community effort that required fortitude as well as endless political negotiation. We bought an ideal lot from Temple Emanuel, on Chandler Street, but encountered tremendous opposition from the neighbors, who took their protest all the way to the Massachusetts Superior Court. We gained, lost and regained our funding from the Department of Housing and Urban Development (HUD). I was at the front and center of this arduous process, fraught with obstacles, challenges, disappointments, doubts and frustration. At last, after a roller coaster of successes and failures, the doors of Bet Shalom opened to the first residents in December 1983.

The original mission of Elder Home Care was to provide in-home services to frail, low-income older people so that they could remain in their homes with dignity and respect. We employed social workers to conduct interviews, create case files and arrange for services for eligible clients. As a case management agency, we didn't provide services ourselves; instead, we contracted out to offer our clients transportation to doctor's appointments or the beauty salon, for example, or homemaker and chore services.

From the very start, Sol threw me right into the pool without hesitation, allowing me to do everything necessary to learn how to run the agency. As a boss, he was both difficult and wonderful. Indeed, on my first day of work, he was on vacation. I had planned to spend the day introducing myself to everyone on the staff, taking the time to speak with each of them to get to know them. Instead, a call came in from the Area Agency on Aging first thing that morning, asking where our proposal was.

"What proposal?" I said.

"The one that was due today."

I begged for a reprieve but was only given until the next morning. I spent a frantic first day with the director of clinical services, adapting the previous year's proposal, changing dates and details, and got it in to the AAA the next day. Every time anyone came near me, I had to say, "Ask me tomorrow." The incident gave me great confidence, but it was terrifying. And it was certainly an indication of what my working life with Sol Boskind was going to be like.

Yet there is no doubt that Sol made it easy for me to learn. He shared all of his knowledge with me. He took me with him when he went into Boston to the Executive Office of Elder Affairs, and he always brought me to meetings of Mass Home Care, the state association to which we belonged. (Although we were a non-profit agency, 98% of our budget came from the state; there were 27 home care agencies like ours.) In the end, I not only did my job but also some of his, in part because he was taking medication for a heart problem and often slept at his desk. The chair of the board, Henry Hemenway, used to call me at home and say, "Lois, I want to run this by you." I would say, "Henry, why aren't you calling Sol?" And he would answer, "Because you know the answer! You're smart and you'll tell me." (Henry invited me to join his men's group, called the Torch Club. It met once a month at WPI, and members took turns giving lectures. I was the only woman.)

As Assistant Director, one of my early responsibilities was to supervise our new elder abuse unit. At the time, we were the demonstration site for a pilot project on elder abuse, funded by the Administration on Aging and headed by Rosalie Wolf, an Elder Home Care board member and a dear friend of mine. The project's goal was to investigate the issue of abuse, with an eye to understanding its nature and extent as well as how to address it. So there I was in a supervisory position, with absolutely no knowledge of the issue. At that point, however, none of us really knew a lot about elder abuse. As a result of the project, we learned that abuse most often came not from a spouse stretched to the breaking point by the strain of caring for an Alzheimer's patient, but from an adult child with mental problems of his or her own. Moreover, older people find it very difficult to talk about abuse. They would rather live in the circumstances they know than separate from the child or caretaker, even if they are being mistreated. In one instance, the supervisor wasn't in, and one of our Protective Services workers had to visit a client who had a real problem with her adult son. He was violent. I went with her myself, taking my umbrella out of the car in case I had to use it as a weapon. All I could think of was how ridiculous it was that I of all people was preparing to defend this elderly woman from an adult perpetrator – with an umbrella.

In another case, we had to go to probate court to secure permission to make an older person safe. The judge said to us, "What is it I am supposed to do?" There were no case laws, no precedents. So we explained, and he made his decision in our favor. That's how elder abuse law developed: case by case. As the initial site, we did a lot of training across the state. Rosalie went on to become a national authority on elder abuse. By the time we finished the demonstration project, the Massachusetts legislature had passed the Elder Abuse Law to protect older adults.

There were times when I was so frustrated that I didn't want to stay at Elder Home Care. At one point, when I had decided that Sol was never going to retire and allow me to step up as Executive Director, I decided to apply to become an Assistant Secretary with Paul Lanzikos, the Secretary of Elder Affairs. Bob thought I was crazy to be thinking about working for the state, in Boston, in my fifties. Nonetheless, I persevered, and the interview process began. At the time, I was suffering from sciatica, and I used to drive back and forth to Boston with an ice pack on my leg, daydreaming about the terrific pad I was going to rent on Beacon Hill when I got the job. It went on for six months, interview after interview. Finally, I went in yet again to meet with the Secretary. By then, it was down to me and one other candidate. Bob and I were due to leave for Florida the next day, and Paul Lanzikos said he wanted to bring me in one more time.

"Paul," I said, "make a decision. Six months is long enough."

We flew to Florida, and the next day he called to tell me they had picked Andy Bader, the other candidate. It was really fine with me. I worked beautifully with and was very fond of Andy.

I did love Sol, even though he frustrated me. He was a great old man, and I was incredibly fond of him. Moreover, knowing my personality, I'm not sure I could have worked under anyone else. In 1985, three years after I had begun at Elder Home Care, he finally retired, and I did become Executive Director. By that time, I knew everything about the job. I remember on Sol's last day, a Friday, he called me into his office. He said, "I know you didn't like my style of management because I left everything to you. I could do it because I knew I would be there in case of an emergency." And I said, "No, Sol, I didn't agree with your approach. But you taught me an incredible amount, and you gave me the freedom to learn it all. For that I am eternally grateful." On Monday morning, I moved in and sat down at his desk as though I had been Executive Director forever.

As the years went on, the state contributed more money to elder care agencies but narrowed the qualifications for care. The philosophy shifted. The goal was still to keep older people in their homes, but it was a different kind of older person. We were now expected to help the really frail, those who could not stay at home at all without our help. The care plans became much more involved. As we added home health services to address the needs of our clients, we no longer had the money to send them to Bingo or to have their hair done. Before I left, after ten years at the agency, we also added nurses to our staff, which really changed the focus. We maintained our original contracts with outside nurses and home health aides, who continued to provide the direct care to our clients. But our own nurses visited homes to determine whether someone was eligible for nursing home placement; they went to nursing homes, meeting with clients who might be ready to return to the community with our help. They also often went out with case managers to investigate concerns about safety. Today, Elder Services has grown exponentially. There is money specifically earmarked for congregant housing and for clients to hire their own help. There are many new programs about which I only know peripherally.

Elder Home Care was a ten-year learning experience for me. One particular incident brought me up short, teaching me my most valuable lesson about the importance of paying attention to process. At the time, I was also on the board of the Visiting Nurses Association (VNA) and very friendly with

Mary Lou McNiff, the head of clinical services there. Medical and social services were then so fragmented that older people often became confused; they didn't know who was coming in to visit them or when. Frequently, a caseworker from Elder Home Care and a nurse from the VNA would end up visiting the same client at different times on the same day. Mary Lou and I thought it would be wonderful to coordinate care so that a case manager and a nurse could arrive at the home together. We wrote a grant outlining such a plan and were funded.

Our approach was way ahead of our time, and we were thrilled. I went back to my agency and announced the new plan to our case managers. Mary Lou sat her nurses down and told them. Both groups were furious. Now, on any given day, they were going to have to arrange their schedules with each other instead of planning on their own to line up a series of visits to clients. Our coordinated care plan was discussed in the state legislature for its innovative quality, but it didn't matter. My staff didn't want to follow it, and they dragged their feet.

I will never forget the day I met with the supervisors. I had slipped and fallen and hurt my back; I was leaving for Florida the next day for a week's vacation. They asked to see me before I left, and all six of them let me have it with both barrels about how difficult I had made their jobs. I got on the plane for Florida and thought about it for a solid week. And I realized how wrong I had been. In hindsight, I understood that we should have either assigned a case manager to the VNA to work on the project with a nurse, or vice versa.

I learned that it was essential to meet with the supervisors whenever I had an opportunity to do something new. I needed to ask them what they thought, what the issues were and how we might overcome them -- together. I learned the hard way that process takes longer, but when you get the commitment of the staff, it's a win-win situation. In my volunteer world, I knew very well that you could never move in a new direction unless the volunteers were willing to follow. But somehow, in this instance, I had become so carried away with this new opportunity – and perhaps with my own authority – that I lost my common sense.

Of course, I didn't always take the time to rely on process. Sometimes I had to make a major decision quickly, and on my own. When Lou Swan came on as assistant director of Elder Home Care (he succeeded me in 1991 and has been a wonderful Executive Director ever since), he told me I too often short-circuited the process. He had been Executive Director of the Age Center, but he had agreed to move to Elder Home Care as an assistant director because he liked the internal details and liked to plan. I would get a call from the Office of Elder Affairs because they knew I always got things done. I would say, "Okay, Lou, this is what we're doing." And he would say, "Lois, you always jump to do something without figuring out all of the things that could happen or what could go wrong." I would answer, "Lou, I agreed to do it. It's your job now to figure out how to get it done." Lou was so great as the inside person. His expertise allowed me to be active in Worcester and at the state level on aging issues. I remember visiting the State House, sitting on the desk of our representative Kevin O'Sullivan, discussing legislation. That is also where I met Mary Jane McKenna, who is now my neighbor at the Seasons.

It's always been difficult for me to plan. I prefer to just do! I think quickly and get to the end quickly. It is dreadfully difficult for me to sit with a group of people who are planning something when I can already envision the outcome. It was even worse years later, when I served as President and CEO of the United Way. There was so much planning, and I had so little time. There is a place for planning, but you can also plan to death. I like action. That's just who I am. If I think it's important to get something done, I say yes, and then I figure out how to do it. Not a lot of people think that way.

In the late 1980s, when I ran Elder Home Care, I also served as chairman of the board of directors at the United Way. I was constantly changing hats. On the third Tuesday of every month at noon, I met with my board of directors as Executive Director of Elder Home Care, where I supported the chairman of the board. Then, at four p.m. that same afternoon, I went to the United Way's monthly board meeting, where I chaired the meeting and was in turn supported by the organization's executive director. The dual experience gave me a broad perspective in later years, when I was able to serve as a consultant not only for executive directors but also for boards.

I loved my job at Elder Home Care. I couldn't wait to get to the office every single day. When I look back, I do think I really made a difference there. I was particularly proud of my response to personnel issues. One of my concerns was maternity leave. Often, when supervisors or case managers left to have babies, we ended up losing them because we wouldn't allow them to return to work part-time. I stewed and stewed about the issue. Most of our case managers were women in their early thirties. Turnover was high, and we were losing highly qualified people. And so I instituted a new policy of part-time work. I knew it was the right thing to do, but there was a flurry of concern about the new plan. The receptionist was convinced that she would never be able to keep track of who was in and who was out. So I sat down with the supervisors and made a deal with them. I said, "The only way this will work is if you agree to share your case managers on the day you're not in." They all agreed. They were very excited; a few of them were pregnant at the time. We put the most complicated chart out front for the receptionist! This case manager would be in on Monday, Wednesday and Thursday in the morning, another one might be there in the afternoons. One supervisor came in only on Tuesdays and Thursdays. But we never once had a problem.

I also noticed that there was no diversity in our office. We didn't have enough staff members who were Spanish-speaking, even though there were elderly Hispanics in our client base. (Most went back to their countries of origin when they aged.) Moreover, we were an elder care agency, but we employed no older people. When I asked the supervisors what was going on, they said, "Well, we hired an older woman once, and it didn't work out." They meant well, but they were hiring people just like themselves. From that moment on, I asked that every resume cross my desk. I began to flag anyone whom I thought we should interview, and it made a huge difference in our hiring pattern.

We hired some wonderful older people. I was most proud of Barbara Dyson, the receptionist who sat outside my office. She was in her fifties, with grown children. I would hear her talking to the clients. She was superb with them, gentle and insightful. So one day, I asked, "Barbara, would you like to be a case manager?" She said, "Oh, no, I can't. I've never been to college. I'm not qualified." I said, "You're qualified." We trained her to set limits with clients and to develop care plans, and she became one of our best case managers.

When I first became director and began to read through case files, I was appalled at the level of writing, as well as the judgmental language I discovered. I was concerned that if we were to be subpoenaed, as we were occasionally, we would get in considerable trouble in court. As a result, I began to talk to new case managers about how to prepare a case file. I focused on good, clear writing, impartial tone and organization. As the years progressed and more of the case managers and supervisors wanted to pursue master's degrees, they often brought their applications in for me to review. Everybody made fun. They would say, "Don't take it to Lois, she'll make all kinds of corrections."

One young case manager, Juan Gomez, came in to meet with me one day and said, "Lois, I'd like to go back and get my degree." When I asked him what the problem was, he said, "Well, my classes interfere with my work." He was Hispanic and had special clients who required more involvement than others. He took them to appointments and stayed to interpret; he followed up on social security issues with them. I told him, "I think we can work it out." He went on to get his master's degree and ended up on the Worcester City Council. (He invited me to attend his inauguration with his mother.) He is now running Centro Las Americas. I told him that he had to promise me to invite me when he became governor.

I loved the Elder Home Care staff. I always thought of it as a kind of family. My office door was always open. People could come in or out whenever they wanted. I used to go in early and on Saturday mornings to do my own work, so I had more accessibility to the staff during the regular working day. When everybody came in every morning, I walked around to say hello.

I knew who had trouble with a babysitter, whose mother was sick and so forth. If it was a snowy day, they brought their children in to work with them. I ran the agency in a different kind of way.

The state often slashed our budget, forcing us to cut services and refrain from taking any new clients. Some home cares didn't reduce their services in such circumstances, but we ran our agency prudently so that we came out on budget at the end of the fiscal year. As a result, when the legislature passed a supplemental budget in the spring every year, we received less money, and agencies that had been less frugal were rewarded with expanded budgets. It was always a conundrum for the board and for me, but the board would not allow us to spend money we didn't have.

At the end of June in 1991, the budget was so bad that I had to cut ten case managers from the staff. We met at our usual Wednesday staff meeting, and I had to tell them there was bad news. I had to figure out who could stay and who had to go. They said to me, "Lois, we trust you, but could you tell us before the Fourth of July? We don't want to wait."

So, on a horrendous day right before the Fourth, I sat in my office and gave my secretary, Carol, the names of the ten most recently hired. One by one, they walked into my office, and I had to tell them they were let go. I asked them to consider coming back if the budget improved. They cried. I cried. Almost everyone said they felt bad for me for having to choose. Nobody blamed me. I had always shared information with them at our staff meetings. They knew when the budget wasn't good. I didn't hide things from them. That evening, when Bob came home, I was lying on the couch and he said, "Are you all right?" I said, "No. I've had the saddest day, and I am exhausted." Not long afterwards, I had begun to plan for the annual meeting in November when I said to myself, "This is enough. I'm tired, and I'm going to move on." I was 61 years old. They gave me a wonderful farewell, held at Bet Shalom, and I retired at the beginning of December.

I am still very attached to Elder Services. Even though I haven't worked there since 1991, I still refer to the agency as "we." I stay in contact with the staff that is still there. Every fall, when I teach a two-week Geriatric Clerkship for medical and graduate nursing students at UMass, I have my students spend two days at Elder Home Care, where they go out on visits with case managers and protective service workers to learn what they do to keep older people at home and safe. Wherever I go, I bump into somebody who used to work at the agency. They are everywhere. I come across them as social workers at Memorial Hospital. One of my former colleagues at Elder Home Care, Theresa Ekstrom, works with me on the Geriatric Clerkship, along with Linda Craigin, a long-time colleague from Memorial Hospital. When I take my students to Notre Dame Nursing Home, I meet with a social worker who used to be one of the supervisors. The person who gives me chemo has a sister who once sat across the hall from me at Elder Home Care.

Sometimes I rue the fact that I left. I would like to have seen the agency grow and develop into the kind of work it does now. But there comes a time to move on. When I begin to find annual meetings too tedious and board meetings too boring to arrange, then it is time to go. And in my extraordinary life, every time a door has closed, another has opened. I have never regretted a decision to move on. I never wanted to outstay my welcome.

That winter, I retired for approximately two weeks. I hated

it. I didn't want to go shopping. I didn't want to sit around the house. I didn't want to play cards.

And one morning during those two weeks, somebody called me and said, "You've been both an executive director and a chairman of a board, and I wonder if you could come in and consult with me about some issues I'm having with my board."

I said, "Well, let me think about it."

"And tell us what you charge."

What I charged? I had no idea. I quickly called my daughter in California to ask her, and Sarah gave me some advice.

I called the person back and said, in a squeaky voice, "$75 an hour?"

She said, "Perfect!"

So began sixteen years of consulting to non-profits. I loved it. My knowledge grew as I gained in experience. I went in to agencies to assess management issues; I did strategic planning and leadership training; I ran many, many board trainings on roles and responsibilities. I've mentored executive directors; I've been hired by boards to address concerns about executive directors. I did some work with the Greater Worcester Community Foundation, helping with their non-profit support center. The Boys and Girls Club followed my strategic plan exactly, building a wonderful club in Main South. My advice to them had been to focus on that neighborhood, where the organization provided a safe haven for children. At the groundbreaking, I was so moved by the work they had done and that I had played a role in it. The last board training I did was for Becker College in 2008, where I had also received an honorary degree. Two years ago, I turned over all of my requests for consultation work to my close friend and colleague, Patsy Lewis. At this point, I primarily give free advice. I want the freedom not to be tied down anymore.

In essence, I never really retired. I just redirected my energies. At the same time, I continued to stay involved with all of my activities in the community and found life very fulfilling. Bob was, as he had always been, a vital part of that fulfillment.

"To Those I Love"

If I should ever leave you whom I love
to go along the silent way,
Grieve not, nor speak of me with tears,
but laugh and talk of me as if I were
beside you there.

I'd come – I'd come, could I but find a way!
But would not tears and grief be barriers?
And when you hear a song or see a bird I loved,
please do not let the thought of me be sad ...
For I am loving you just as I always have ...
you were so good to me!

There are so many things I wanted still to do –
So many things to say to you...
Remember that I did not fear ...
It was just leaving you that was so hard to face ...
We cannot see Beyond ... But this I know:
I love you so – 'twas heaven here with you!

- Isla Paschal Richardson

CHAPTER SIX

"MR. LOIS GREEN"

There is no question in my mind, not even an inkling of a doubt, that I could never have accomplished what I have without Bob. There probably were few men of his generation who would have willingly given me the space, the time and the support both physically and emotionally to do what I wanted and needed to do. He was always there. As I think back over the years, at all the things I have achieved, he deserves much of the credit.

Bob grew up in a family of modest means on Worcester's East Side, which was heavily Jewish in those days. Today, the Jewish community has fully shifted to the West Side of the city, carrying with it the synagogues and Jewish institutions. Before World War II, however, only the well-to-do could afford to move. The Greens lived on North Woodford Street, parallel to Providence Street, on the second floor of a three-decker. Bob always said he never thought much about not having a lot of money, as everyone on the East Side lived in the same circumstances. His father,

Irving, sold insurance, and his mother, Belle, worked in Sherer's Department Store. He had a younger brother, Arthur, and a baby sister, Elaine, who was nine years younger. Elaine told me that when Bob was born, he was considered the golden boy and was always beautifully dressed. The children shared a bedroom to make room for a boarder, Mike, who ultimately married Belle's sister, Marion. They were a loving family and often drove down to Woonsocket to visit Aunt Beck and Uncle Sam and their children, with whom Bob remained close even after we were married. A number of years ago, he attended an East Side reunion and had the most wonderful evening. People returned from all over the country to see old friends and neighbors.

Bob loved his childhood, and he and I frequently drove over to the East Side so he could reminisce about his growing up years. He told me how the Polish kids constantly accosted him and his best buddies, Lester and Jack, on the way to *Cheder* (Hebrew School). They paid an older boy, Sid Levy, who was much bigger, to walk beside them for protection. My favorite story was about the paper route he had when he was young. He convinced his little brother, Arthur, to get up at the crack of dawn to deliver the papers as Bob slept. But, on Sundays, it was Bob who collected the money, giving Arthur only a pittance. When Bob was older and moved on to selling ice cream from a truck pulled by a pony, he negotiated the price of the paper route before selling it to his brother. During the war years, when grease was a much-needed commodity, he convinced Arthur to go door-to-door, asking for "elbow grease" for the war effort.

Bob worked his entire life. When he retired a few years before he died, I used to ask him if he missed going to work. And each time he said, "No, I worked my whole life, and I'm going to enjoy every minute of retirement."

Before I met him, Bob had served as an infantryman in World War II. He had enlisted in 1943, on his eighteenth birthday. A year later, not long after D-day, he shipped out to France. After several months of driving supply trucks for Patton's 3rd Army, he was sent to the front lines where, on his first day of combat, he was shot in the face. Somewhere, I have a folder of his Army papers, including a terrible picture of him right after he had been wounded. I hid it from my children because he never wanted them to see it. He spent over a year in the hospital in California, recovering from his wounds, and then returned home. For quite some time, he was on full disability. Thanks to the passage of the GI Bill of Rights for veterans, he was able to go first to Clark University for his bachelor's degree and then on to the Wharton School for his MBA.

When I first met him, I was startled by the scarring, but only for about a minute. He was so charming and funny that it immediately became unimportant. That was how everybody reacted to him, though he always remained self-conscious about the way he looked. If someone took his picture, he turned that side of his face away from the camera. For years and years, he never talked to me or to any of the children about what had happened to him. At some point after we had been married for a while, he received a letter asking him to meet with a psychiatrist at the Veterans' Hospital to discuss any issues he might still be having about his injuries. They wanted to talk to him about reducing the amount of his disability payment. He said to me, "I'm not going to go. I'm having a wonderful life, and I don't want to go tell them that I need full disability when I don't." He did end up with 75% disability, which was a big chunk of money. A big chunk of money! I think it was about $475 a month. But it was a lot of money to us then.

One day, many years later, he and I were driving back home from Boston, and the radio was on. The announcer mentioned something about that particular date, November 8, and Bob suddenly started to cry. It turned out to be the anniversary of the day he had been shot. Right then, in the car, he told me minute by minute exactly what had happened to him. I had never heard it before, and neither had the children.

After we had grandchildren and Bob had retired, he took a course with Deborah Dwork, Rose Professor of Holocaust History at Clark University, about World War II. She asked him if he would tell the students about his experiences during a class. In his lecture, he described the day he was shot:

> We finally attacked on the morning of November 8, 1944. I remember jumping out of my foxhole, running a few yards, then hitting the ground and firing into a wooded area that supposedly held an enemy machine gun nest. I didn't get far before a bullet struck me in the face. I was conscious and screaming for a medic, when out came a young German with a red cross on his arm. We carried a tin of sulfa powder and a compress bandage on our gun belt and when I pointed to them, he applied them to my face. I stayed awake long enough to see the enemy group come out with their hands over their heads and then I drifted off.
>
> When I awoke I was in a makeshift first aid station and a Catholic priest was kneeling over me, giving me last rites. I screamed at him to stop – not because I

wasn't a Catholic, but because I knew I wasn't going to die!

I took that lecture and sent a copy to each of our grandchildren. For the really young ones, I gave it to their parents to put away for them so they would know about their Pop Pop. He had already shared more with them than he had with me or with our children. Tom Brokaw, in *The Greatest Generation*, captured the essence of just that phenomenon. Most men returning from the war, whether they had been wounded or not, just wanted to get on with their lives. They spoke very little about their experiences, a pattern that repeated itself across region, culture and class. It wasn't until they were older that they began to speak out. Bob, too, found it easier to talk about his war years by the time he had grandchildren.

Many years later, several weeks before he died, he told David the story, and our son described the aftermath of Bob's injuries in the eulogy he gave at his father's funeral:

My father was then sent to a hospital in England. There, for the first time since the battle, he saw himself in the mirror. He saw that the bullet had entered over his lip, gone through his mouth and out the side of his cheek. His jaw was broken, his teeth shattered, a piece of his nose gone, his face swollen beyond recognition. If the bullet's angle had been an inch straighter, he would have been killed. But at the moment, he felt as though his life *had* ended, as though he couldn't go on.

But lying not far from him on his ward was a soldier

bandaged from head to toe, with a gap only for his mouth. The soldier had lost his sight and his hearing, but was able to touch the floor with his hands, and identify people from the unique vibrations they made by walking. The soldier was particularly good at figuring out who were the nurses, calling on them cheerfully to come give him a kiss. Inspired by how that soldier had held on to hope and humor against all odds, my father resolved to recover.

After receiving his MBA, Bob returned to Worcester to start a modest insurance agency, financed by Lou and Hy Small. Eventually, he bought out the Smalls, as well as the Alfred G. Isenberg Agency, but kept the names, calling the business Green, Isenberg & Small. In 1970, he formed another insurance brokerage, IAI, with Bill Sullivan and Bill Carrick. Bob always liked to joke about how a Catholic Irishman, a Protestant and a Jew had gotten together to run a business. They had the most wonderful relationship. It was a new concept of how to do business. Though each had his own insurance business, they shared the back office work. Bob once told David the secret of his business success: "people have to buy insurance from someone, and they're more likely to buy it from someone who is pleasant and fun to be with than someone who is not."

Bob was, of course, committed to his job, but he had made it very clear from the outset that he intended to be an involved father. He absolutely adored the children, and he refused to let work interfere with them, even if it might have meant a more lucrative way of life. When they suffered, he suffered. When they were happy, he was happy. Very warm and unusually sentimental, he cried easily, which most men didn't do. He cried at weddings and bar mitzvahs, and he always hugged. He hugged his son all the time. He taught David that it was okay to be demonstrative, and, as a result, David is just as warm and compassionate as his father was.

When Sarah, our oldest, was born, you would have thought it was the second coming. Bob was ecstatic. She was so smart. At my mother's house, there was a big grandfather clock. When Sarah was only eleven months old, she would run to the clock every time it rang and say, "tick tock." Bob loved to read to her. She would complete the last word of each sentence before he finished.

When I was pregnant with David, he asked me how he could possibly love another child as much as he loved Sarah. I assured him that his love would expand with each child we had. And it did. Patty, number three, came four years later, to his great joy. And Rachel was the only one of the four whose birth he watched. He always called the two youngest his "peanuts," even when they were all grown up. They loved climbing into bed with him on Sunday mornings while he read the funnies to them. This ritual was always followed by a pancake breakfast. Not only did they push me to the very edge of the bed while I was trying to read the paper, but they also made it very clear that they preferred Daddy's breakfasts and lunches on the weekends.

Bob was very close to David, our only son. He used to play basketball with David and his friends in the backyard all the time. On weekends or mild weekday evenings, we could hear the reverberating thump, thump of the ball in the driveway. He and David also used to play one on one, until one day Bob came inside, devastated because David had beaten him! Rachel was the child who most loved the Red Sox. After she turned ten, Bob would take her out of school and to the Red Sox home opener for her birthday, which was in April. One day, they came home early and told me the game had been cancelled because of the cold. They had been chatting all the way into Fenway Park and couldn't believe how easy it had been to park. The parking lot attendant gave them the bad news. But Bob refused to disappoint her. The next day, he took her out of school again, and they went back to Boston for Opening Day.

During the summer, when the children and I went to the beach in Connecticut, he drove down every weekend even though he hated the drive and loathed the rocky beach. He used to say that the elves came every winter to sharpen the stones. But week after week, he came down because the children and I loved it so much. Our biggest weekend treat was going to Jimmy's for hotdogs or hot lobster rolls. We often thought that was Bob's only motivation for coming to the beach.

He was particularly known as a storyteller, a skill he had honed in his younger years when he had worked as a camp counselor. Every night, he told the children in his bunk a story. Because it was a Jewish camp, he started at the ending and worked backwards to the beginning. If he were going to tell a story about a baseball game, he would start with the final score and go backwards until he reached the first pitch of the first inning. He used to tell me that all of the other counselors would get their own campers to bed and then race over to Bob's bunk so they could hear the stories told backwards.

He loved telling his own children stories. Their favorite story was about Debbie Cubicha-Cubicha Kowski and Marvin the Bear, and Bob told it over and over again. Although Debbie's parents have warned her never to go into the woods, one day she decides to journey past the edge of the trees. She gets lost, and Marvin the Bear finds her and brings her home. Her parents are so happy to have her back, and Debbie never goes into the woods again! Sometimes, Bob would try to tell a different story, but all of the children would say, "No, no, we want the Debbie Cubicha-Cubicha Kowski and Marvin the Bear story!" All of the nieces and nephews loved his stories, too.

When our grandson, Alex, Patty's son and older child, was in kindergarten, grandparents were asked to volunteer to come into the classroom. The morning that Bob and I went in, I was scheduled to speak in the afternoon at a hearing at the legislature on Beacon Hill. As we were driving to Alex's school in Wayland, Bob asked, "Are you nervous?"

"I can't tell you how nervous I am," I said. "You'll laugh at me."

"But you've spoken so many times!"

"Oh, I'm not nervous about the hearing," I told him. "I'm nervous that they're going to give me some craft thing to do in kindergarten, and I'm going to make a fool of myself."

We laughed, but it turned out that my assignment was to help the children make Mother's Day cards. My worst nightmare! And what did they ask Bob to do? Tell stories!

In the kindergarten room, there was an arts and crafts table, a computer area, a reading nook, a storytelling corner etc. and the children could move from one station to another. There I sat in utter terror at the arts and crafts table, trying to help the kids even though I couldn't even cut straight.

The teacher came over to me and said, "None of the children

are at their stations. They're all in the corner listening to your husband. Could he come all the time?"

And I thought, "Well, you're certainly never going to ask me to come back again."

Bob loved children. He played constantly with our nine grandchildren, as well as with nieces, nephews and neighborhood children. He pulled quarters out of their ears or introduced them to the trap game, where he trapped a child between his legs, pretended to fall asleep and then allowed them to escape. One of his favorite traditions was to play Simon Says. He would begin slowly and then increase the speed until everyone was out. They loved it, and so did he.

Bob delighted in telling me outrageous tales, which I always believed. After all, I thought, why would a husband tell a wife something that wasn't true? Two tall tales stand out even all these years later. The first was "the road story." When we had been married about two months, we drove from Worcester to visit my grandmother in Colchester, Connecticut. A new road was being built, and off to the side was the old, curvy road.

"Oh, isn't it sad," I said to Bob, just to make conversation with my new husband. "They're never going to use that road again. It will just lie there."

He was driving. "That's not true, Lois," he said. "In Connecticut, when they make a new road, they call the State Road Warehouse. They come with a big steamroller, roll up the old road and put it in a warehouse. Then when they need a new road someplace, they use the old road."

And I said, "Gee, I never knew that!"

He said, "Well, of course!"

This was really interesting information, and I tucked it

away for future reference.

A number of years later, we were driving back home from Boston with two other couples after a night at the theater. Driving along Route 9 – the Mass Turnpike hadn't yet been built -- we passed through Framingham, where once again we saw an abandoned road next to a new road under construction.

And I, in my most authoritative voice, said to our friends, "You know, in Connecticut, they would have called the warehouse and brought out one of those old roads."

Of course, they nearly howled me out of the car.

Bob's brother worked for a big company that built roads. He went to a convention in Chicago and reported later that somebody had stood up to tell a story about a young woman who believed that the old roads were rolled up and stored away. The place was hysterical. So that story reached a national audience.

Many years later, when Mount Pleasant Country Club and its golf course were in the process of being built, Bob and I used to drive to Boylston to watch the progress. One Sunday when we visited, all of the greens had been laid out, and by the next week they had all been put in.

I said to Bob, "My God, I never saw grass grow so fast."

He said, "Lois, there's a farm in New Hampshire where they grow grass. They roll it up, transport it and then put it in."

I looked at him and said "I fell for that shit a long time ago, but don't think you're going to get me to believe it now."

And, of course, that time he was telling the truth.

The other story that still makes people laugh happened when the children were little. I drove a Chevrolet station wagon. We lived right off Salisbury Street, and I had to drive up a fairly steep hill from Park Avenue. I was an aggressive driver and always wanted to be the first out of the gate at the intersection below.

One day, I came home and said to Bob, "You know, I'd like a new car."

"Why?" he said. "Isn't the car big enough for the four kids and the dog?"

"Oh, yes, it's really fine," I answered.

"So what's the matter with it?"

"It doesn't have enough pickup."

"Okay," he said. "You don't need a new car. This one is a six cylinder. Call the Chevrolet people, and tell them you want to bring the car in and have them put in more cylinders. And if you're not happy with an eight cylinder, they'll put in a ten cylinder."

I said, "I didn't know you could do that."

"Well, you wouldn't. You don't know that much about cars."

So I called the Chevrolet dealer, and was asked, "Mrs. Green, what can we do for you?"

I said, "Well, my car doesn't have a lot of pickup, so I'd like to bring it in and have you add two more cylinders."

The man laughed so hard he had to put down the receiver.

I fell for Bob's preposterous stories over and over again.

He had the most wonderful sense of humor. Someone might ask him, "Gee, Bob, I'd like you to play in my golf tournament because I'm raising money for such and such a cause." Bob would say, "I'll be out of town. When is it?" He was so quick. When he became president of Temple Emanuel, he would sometimes go out drinking with his buddies and stay out late. I'd say to him, "You can't do that. You're president of Temple now." He would say, "Lois, that's why I'm going out. It's very important for me to understand how some members of the congregation might behave if they're in trouble. Now I can understand."

Bob used to irritate me because he had such a good disposition. If he lost a client at work, I would be so upset, yet the next Saturday there he would be out on the green, playing golf with the same man. I'd say, "Aren't you angry with him?" And he would answer, "Why should I be angry with him? If he found a better deal, then all the more power to him."

At times, I was the bane of his existence. He loved to tell me about something that had happened. And when he described it, he went from A to B to C. I would wait patiently for about two minutes, and then I would say, "Oh, and so this happened?" He would say to me, "It's so irritating when you do that. And it's even more irritating when you're right."

We didn't often make a big deal for birthdays, but when he turned 70, I asked him what he would like.

"Oh, I don't need anything," he answered.

"No, really," I pressed. "This is a big birthday."

He thought for a minute. "Well," he said, "What I'd really like is to be able to finish a sentence."

I just looked at him. "You're pushing it," I told him.

Bob was never in a hurry to get anywhere, nor did he care how he got there. For years, I fumed whenever we had to go through a tollbooth on the highway together. I was certain that Bob deliberately got in the longest line just to aggravate me. When I drove myself, I would count every car in every line as I approached. If there was a truck, that was worth two cars. Then I chose the shortest and quickest line. I was furious if a driver ahead of me dropped his change and held me up even a few seconds longer.

When I was in my fifties, I took the Myers-Briggs Type Indicator to figure out my personality type. It described me as an ENTJ, or Extraverted iNtuitive Thinking Judging:

> ENTJs are natural born leaders. They live in a world of possibilities where they see all sorts of challenges to be surmounted, and they want to be the ones responsible for surmounting them. They have a drive for leadership, which is well served by their quickness to grasp complexities, their ability to absorb a large amount of impersonal information, and their quick and decisive judgments. They are 'take charge' people. (http://www.personalitypage. com/ENTJ.html)

When I came home to share the results with Bob, he laughed. "Well, what did you learn? Obviously not much about yourself, because we already know what your personality is."

I said, "I owe you an apology. For all these years, I thought you were getting in the longest line at the toll booths because you were being passive aggressive. I finally realized that you only did it because it was the closest!" It had never even dawned on him to consider whether a line was longer or shorter.

We had a wonderful marriage, but we argued just like any other couple. The difference between us was that I'd stop talking to him, and he would merrily continue to talk to me as though nothing had happened. He would tell me goodbye in the morning and go off to the office. That night, he would come home and ask, "How's everything?" Inevitably, he would say something funny and make me laugh. After a few days of trying not to speak to him, I would say to myself, "Well, the only one I'm punishing here is myself." I couldn't be angry and laugh at the same time. What fun was that? Once, we were arguing while we were driving in the car, and I asked him if he wanted a divorce. He said, "No, I can't, because I would remarry, and she would think that I could make a decision."

There was one area where neither of us would compromise, and that was politics. Bob was a Republican, and I was a fiscally conservative bleeding heart liberal. Politically, we were always at war. One morning, the newspaper didn't arrive. Bob, who wasn't gripped by politics the way I was, asked if it was Election Day. Without a moment's hesitation, I said to him, "Oh, no, it's next week." Off he went to the office while I dashed out to the polls to have my vote count for the first time without being cancelled by his!

About six-thirty that night, he appeared at the back door and stood there with his arms folded.

I looked up at him and said, "Well, it was worth a try."

We both laughed. At 5:30 that evening, he had been about to leave for the day when his secretary asked him if he had voted. When he said, "No, Election Day isn't till next week," she had told him, "Someone is pulling your leg."

In 1968, when Bob voted for Richard Nixon, I put two extra leaves in the table and put the four children and me at one end and Bob all alone at the other end. I told the kids that he needed to be ostracized because he had voted the wrong way.

But we managed to survive all of our differences. He even let me put signs on the lawn for my candidates, though he did complain that he was never allowed his own turn.

It is difficult to imagine a more supportive husband than

he was, particularly given the culture of the times. Not only did Bob want me to pursue my dreams, but he also told me that I was a wonderful mother and balanced family and work well. In 1952, when we were married, he believed that ours was a partnership. He never resented me. As my son, David, said in the eulogy at Bob's funeral, "he never felt eclipsed; he felt enlarged."

He was very involved in the Worcester community himself. Not only was he a leader at Temple Emanuel, but he also served as a trustee at Hahnemann Hospital, taught at Clark and was on the board at the Youth Guidance Center. At Mount Pleasant, he was a fixture virtually from its beginning. He was so comfortable in his own skin – and so secure about our marriage – that he was perfectly sanguine about my own public role. Once, Alex Drapos, a local lawyer and civic leader, introduced him to a man who hadn't met him before.

"I'm so sorry," said the man, as he held out his hand to Bob. "I don't think I know you."

"Yes, you do," Alex told him. "That's Mr. Lois Green."

"Oh!" responded the man. "Of course!"

We made a deal early on that he would go only to the events that mattered to me – an annual meeting, if I was speaking, or a presentation in which I was involved. He didn't mind being in my limelight, but he preferred not to go if I didn't need him. Most of the time, it was boring for him. When I was involved in the Council of Jewish Federations, a few of those quarterly meetings across the country were held in interesting places. At first, we thought it would be fun if he went with me. But it didn't work out very well. My meetings took up a lot of time, and I was often busy; he had to wait around for me. So we decided that we would rather travel by ourselves, when I could devote the time.

At the same time, he shared everything that mattered to me. One Saturday when I was in the middle of overseeing the building of Bet Shalom, Bob was leaving the house to go to the office for a few hours and then play golf.

"What are you doing today?" he asked. He rarely asked when he was off to the office.

"I'm not going to tell you," I said. "You'll get mad at me."

"No, I won't get mad. I promise."

So I said, "Well, I don't like the bricks they picked for Bet Shalom. The architect gave me pictures of three buildings in and around Boston. I'm going with my camera to take pictures of the one that has the bricks I like best."

"Oh, for God's sake," he said, "you are impossible." He went out, slammed the door, got in his car, backed out of the driveway, drove back in the driveway, came in the back door and said, "I'll take you."

Bob was there for me - and for all of us. As our children grew up and into their own lives, he remained close to them and to every one of his grandchildren. They adored their Pop-pop, and he them. Every time a grandchild was born, Bob wrote the name, date, weight and how the mother was doing on a scrap of paper and tucked it beneath the glass top on his bureau. When he was dying, I stayed up night after night, putting together an album full of pictures with Bob and me and the grandchildren and gave it to him at a big family party on his birthday. I put each of those little bits of paper at the front of the album.

Our oldest, Sarah, lives in Los Angeles and is a story analyst for 20th Century Fox, where she works in feature film development, reading books and scripts for their five different film divisions. Her husband, Ken Durkin, is an art teacher at an inner city high school in LA. He's also a wonderful artist. I have his paintings in both Worcester and Florida; in fact, in Florida, his is the only artwork I have hanging. They have two boys, Jesse and Gabriel.

I see bits and pieces of Bob in each of the children, but I probably see the most of him in David. I can't imagine David's having an enemy in the world. He is caring, warm, emotional; he just wants to be with his family. He has the same quick sense of humor as his father, the same personality. Once, when David was coming home for Thanksgiving while he was in law school, Bob and I went to the airport to pick him up. On the night before Thanksgiving, Logan was crowded and chaotic, filled with travelers flying in and out. David didn't appear. We finally got a message that he had missed the plane and would be arriving first thing the next morning. We had to come back to get him.

By the time he got off the plane the next day, I was furious. "David," I asked, "what happened?"

"Well," he said, "I got to the airport late, and the gate had already closed. The woman behind the counter said, 'Mr. Green, you were supposed to be here twenty minutes before the plane took off.'"

"What did you say?" I asked.

"I said, 'Oh! Twenty minutes BEFORE the plane took off!'"

We burst out laughing, and that was the end of it. We quote that line often. It was such a Bob thing for him to say.

Somewhere in my memorabilia is a pair of letters. The first, from Bob to his own father, was about how he was managing his money when he was in graduate school. In that same folder, Bob saved a letter that David wrote him about he was managing his money. I don't think David knows that his father saved those two letters, written a generation apart.

David had Bob's gift of gab as well as his sense of humor. He had a tiny Chevrolet Chevette that he named Howard. After he graduated from college and before he started law school, he drove Howard off to Seattle to seek his fortune. While he was there, Howard's clutch broke. David tried to get it fixed, but it was past warranty and the repairs were going to cost a lot of money. So he sat down to write a letter to the manufacturer, saying, "I would like to know that General Motors, one of the largest corporations in the world, is big enough to stand behind its smallest car, and pay for the cost of replacing such an obviously defective part." A few weeks later, General Motors wrote back and agreed to pay for Howard's repairs.

David is now a lawyer in Washington D.C. He is Vice President for Public Policy at NBC Universal, where he focuses on policy issues relating to protecting digital content from theft. His wife, Wendy Zevin, is a clinical psychologist. They have two children, Jeremy and Andrea. At the beginning of their marriage, they lost two children, Eli and Molly, to the genetic illness, Canavan's Disease, which primarily affects Jews. It was probably the most devastating moment of Bob's and my own married life when we learned that Eli had been born with Canavan's. We were heartbroken when he died at the age of eighteen months. To watch your children in pain is one of the worst things parents face, and we ached for David and Wendy, just as they ached for Eli.

To our disbelief, Molly, who was born shortly after Eli's

death, was affected with the same gene. She died nine months later. I often wonder how anyone recovers from the loss of one child, let alone two. Yet David and Wendy managed their grief and moved bravely on. Thank God they had two wonderful, healthy children after that. Bob and I always held Eli and Molly close to our hearts.

Our third child, Patty, is a preschool head teacher in Wayland, Massachusetts. It's absolutely the most perfect job for her, and she loves it. When she was little, I always said that, of all of my children, she was the one who should have 100 of her own. She took care of Rachel all the time. Before becoming a teacher, she worked with older people who were remaining at home, in an agency similar to Elder Home Care, and then became a private geriatric care manager. You need similar skills, working with either children or older people, and Patty is wonderful at interacting with both age groups. Her husband, Richard Vancil, runs the Executive Advisory Group at IDC where he consults to heads of Sales and Marketing at large IT companies. They have two children, Alex and Laura.

Rachel, our youngest, has a graduate certificate in Management Information Systems from Columbia University. She has co-authored a book, *Mothers-in-law Do Everything Wrong: M.I.L.D.E.W.,* and has spoken on radio shows across the country. She is also involved in many community activities. Her husband, Richard Latto, is managing director of Longroad Asset Management, LLC, which buys distressed companies. They live in Greenwich, Connecticut with their three children, Sammy, Rebecca (or Becca) and Daniel.

In addition to my four children, four in-law children and nine grandchildren, I also have four grand-dogs! The grandchildren all call me "Mocha," a name that originated with Alex when he was only two. At the time, he could say "Mommy," "Daddy," and "Pop-pop" but not "Gammy." So I harassed him every time I saw him.

"Who's that?" I would ask him, pointing to Patty.

"Mommy!" he would say.

"Who's that?" and I pointed to Rich.

"Daddy!"

"Who's that?" I waved at Bob.

"Pop-pop."

And lastly I would point to myself and ask, "Who's this?"

Dead silence.

He knew only one other word, "Mocha-juice" for orange juice. One day, after months of trying to get him to say "Gammy" with no success, I tried once more.

"Who's this, Alex?"

After a struggle, he blurted out, "Mocha!"

From then on he called me Mocha. When he was in day care, I picked him up, and another child asked him who I was. He responded, "Mocha, my grandmutter." He did understand my relationship to him. When he was in kindergarten, he introduced me as Mocha, his favorite flavor.

And so the name stuck. One by one, the other grandchildren as well as the neighbors' children all began to call me Mocha. As the years passed, the entire family co-opted the name. I am now called Mocha, Mockey, the Moch, Mochaccino and sometimes even Mocha Latte. I respond to all and love it.

Bob and I have always thought of our children as wonderful parents, every one of them. I'm very proud of them for being able to balance their families and their work. The siblings are very close. Bob helped to encourage them to stay in touch with each other after they left home. When each child went off to college, he gave them a telephone credit card and told them they could use it either to call home or each other.

And, by bringing the children and their families down to Longboat Key for Thanksgiving every year, we have also helped the cousins develop close relationships, even though most of them live far apart.

By the early 1980s, all four children had graduated from college. Sarah went to Sarah Lawrence as well as to the School of Journalism at the University of California at Berkeley. David graduated from Oberlin College and the University of Pennsylvania Law School. Patty went to Connecticut College. Rachel graduated from the University of Pennsylvania and then went on to Columbia. Bob and I began to travel on our own. In 1982, we went down to Florida to visit my mother, who had a house in Hollywood, on the east coast. Bob wanted to see what the west coast of Florida looked like, and so we first drove over to stay for a couple of days in Longboat Key, in Sarasota County. We visited Fort Myers and Naples and then drove to my mother's. Bob had left his heart not in San Francisco, but in Longboat Key. During the next several years, we returned to stay there, either by ourselves or with Bob's sister, Elaine, and her husband, Charlie.

In 1987, we bought a condo on Longboat Key in Beachplace, the same complex where we had been renting. When Bob first suggested it, I cried and cried, protesting that we were both working full-time. We couldn't afford it; we would never be able to use it; we would never take another vacation anywhere else; and the children would never come. He rarely insisted, but he did this time, and it was the best decision we could have made.

For most of those twenty years, we went back and forth between Worcester and Longboat Key. I was running Elder Home Care, Bob had his office, and I had to take care of my mother, but we went as often as we could. I had four weeks of vacation, and we took three separate weeks in Florida during the winter, a week a month with two weekends. For years, we also went down on the Fourth of July for ten days, which we loved. When Bob retired, he wanted to move down there, at least for the winter, but we never did. I never thought I could stand to be away from home for so long. I have always felt a little bad because it was only after Bob died that I began to spend six months of the year there. Even then, I've only gone for the past two years.

In 1999, Bob and I began to bring all of our family down to Florida for Thanksgiving, a tradition that I have continued on my own. We also have Elaine and Charlie and sometimes their children, Julie and Michele, to whom we are all close, and their grandchildren. In addition, I invite friends or neighbors who have no family around. When I grew up, our Thanksgivings were always at my Aunt Min's house. She invited a house full of people who were not related, and so I have always thought Thanksgiving was all about sharing with those who had no place to go.

Our annual family reunion is so wonderful that it's hard to describe it. My children live all over the country. The siblings and the in-laws all get along beautifully, and the grandchildren can't wait for November every year. As a matter of fact, last August when a couple of the families were together, the grandchildren were already counting how many days it would be until they came to Florida. We are building new memories and traditions, establishing a pattern of family for the grandchildren. We do the same thing every single year. On Wednesday night, we go to a Japanese restaurant. Thursday is Thanksgiving. On Friday, we go out for Italian food, and on Saturday, we bring in pizza. Bob would have loved every minute of it.

I would guess that there wasn't a single person who ever had a bad thing to say about Bob. He died in September of 2001, but everywhere I go, someone has a warm and funny Bob Green story to tell me. He even maintained his sense of humor during his last four months. Everybody who came to the house enjoyed visiting him. He was funny and cute, and his doctors loved him. So did all of the aides. That's just the kind of person he was. He really lives on because he touched so many lives. Nine months after he died, I sold the house on Rutland Terrace and moved to The Seasons in Holden. But this house, too, is full of him. There are photographs everywhere. In the den, I have his purple heart framed and the flag that went over his coffin in a case.

My only regret about our lives together is that he always wanted to travel, and I always seemed to have a commitment that prevented me from going away. Either I was chairing the hospital board, or I was going to speak somewhere, or I had promised the children I would be someplace with them, and I didn't want to leave them or go back on my promise. But Bob never complained. He just said, "Okay, when you can, we'll talk about it."

As our 50th wedding anniversary approached, I said to him, "Bob, now is the time. Where would you like to go?" We put together a trip that was outrageously expensive, something we both really wanted to do. We planned to spend three weeks traveling to Hong Kong and China and Bali and Thailand and Singapore. Scheduled for the end of August in 2001, the trip couldn't have been more exciting. But in April that spring, I was diagnosed with breast cancer and, just six weeks later, Bob was diagnosed with terminal lung cancer. And we had to cancel our plans.

As I think back, it seems to me that Bob was always there for me, and that I always came first. That's the way our entire married life seemed to be. I was the taker, and he was the giver. He never made me feel guilty about it, never made me feel bad. We did travel. The trips we took were wonderful trips. But it wasn't easy to organize my life to get away. Once, when I was ill, I had to cancel a big speaking engagement and find somebody to replace me. "You know," Bob told me, "when something comes up and you have to let somebody down, it's really okay. You're not irreplaceable. But to me, you are."

Shortly before he died, Bob told me that he was not worried about me after he was gone because I was so strong and independent. He would never know how much I depended on him for his strength, his humor, his kindness, his support and his love. Bob was the pillar I leaned on.

CHAPTER SEVEN

HITTING MY STRIDE

"I am of the opinion that our lives belong to the community and that as long as we shall live, it is our privilege to do for it whatever we can. I want to be thoroughly used up when I die, for the harder I work, the more I live. Life is no brief candle for me but a splendid torch that I have hold of for one moment in time, and I want to make it burn as brightly as possible before handing it on to future generations."

- George Bernard Shaw

A lthough my career path became well established in the 1980s, carrying me from working with the mentally ill and challenged into elder care, I continued to devote myself to a parallel track in the volunteer world. Indeed, I never stopped volunteering. Throughout this period, I remained active in the Jewish community, serving as Vice President of both the Worcester Jewish Federation and the Jewish Home (now the Jewish Healthcare Center) and on the board of trustees of Temple Emanuel. In 1982, I chaired the Endowment Fund at Temple, working closely with Rabbi Stanley Davids. My commitment to Bet Shalom extended long past its initial construction and, indeed, has continued until the present day: in the fall of 2008, I gave a speech at the celebration of its twenty-fifth anniversary.

As mentioned earlier, I also served on the board of the Age Center of Worcester as well as the Visiting Nurses Association (VNA) board and the Worcester City Commission on Elder Affairs, positions that complemented my interest in services for older people. My involvement with the United Way has never faltered since my participation in that first campaign in the late 1950s. During this later period, I was on the board for nine years, from 1984 to 1993, as assistant treasurer and chairman of allocations, until in 1988 I became chairman of the board. The first task facing me was to resolve an issue with the Executive Director, a difficult and painful process left to me by the previous chairman, who had not wanted to deal with the problem.

In 1980, my acceptance of a position on the board of the Worcester County Institution of Savings, or WCIS, marked a new beginning of sorts, as I found myself serving the community in a variety of different ways.

At the end of my first meeting at WCIS, they handed me an envelope. When I got home, I opened it, and there was a check for one hundred dollars in it. I was flabbergasted.

"Why did they give me money?" I asked Bob.

He said, laughing, "You're on a corporate board. You get

paid."

"Why didn't I know this?" I asked. "And why am I not on other corporate boards?"

Unfortunately, WCIS was my first and only such experience. As in other endeavors, when it came to the bank board, I was determined that I wasn't going to be one of the boys. I was certain that my signature talents as a woman would be put to better use than if I had tried to behave like a man. Before every board meeting, I considered carefully what I was going to wear. The men always wore black or navy pinstriped suits, with conservative ties. In contrast, I wore a pink or a red suit.

When the Board was told that the hours of the bank's tellers were to be cut, I raised my hand. "Aren't most of the tellers single mothers?" I asked. "If you cut their hours, what will happen to their health benefits?" As a result, the hours were increased to allow at least some benefits. Standing up for the tellers followed my basic instincts of fairness and rights for women. All my life, I understood how women and girls worked together. I learned those kinds of relationships in prep school and college. I always knew that women were more collaborative and didn't seek the same kind of power as men.

In 1982, I joined the board of Mechanics Hall, and in 1985 I helped to found the Worcester Municipal Research Bureau (now the Worcester Regional Research Bureau). The latter organization was an independent organization whose goal was to examine the city's most glaring problems with an eye to providing information and research for possible solutions.

Two years later, I was nominated to become one of four trustees of the Hoche Scofield Foundation, a position I still hold. The other current trustees are Warner Fletcher, Harry

Dewey and the Bank of America. Our fiduciary responsibility is to distribute the interest on the foundation's endowment, resulting in gifts of approximately half a million dollars every year. We focus on significant contributions to health, education and social services. The camaraderie and challenges of the decision-making process as we evaluate proposals, choosing which projects to fund, has been a wonderful experience for me.

I had been involved with Clark University over the years, receiving my MPA there, and serving on a priority task force as a capital campaign was being planned. In the mid-1990s, I was asked if I would be willing to be nominated for the alumni trustee ballot. I agreed and won. I was delighted to be a member of the Board, whose members were committed and dedicated to Clark's success. I chaired the Governance Committee and served as Vice Chairman. After ten years and two terms, I took the required year off and am now an honorary trustee.

Over the years, I developed a certain degree of power, both in terms of the positions I held and the authority with which my opinions were solicited. I didn't gain that kind of influence as a result of giving major contributions. Instead, it came from being respected and trusted. People knew that if they asked me to do something, I would do it. Moreover, I would be fair.

In the same way that one opportunity had always led to another in my life, I found that each role I assumed inevitably led to another, even more interesting experience.

In this way, I ended up becoming deeply involved with Memorial Hospital and, eventually, in its merger with the University of Massachusetts Clinical System. One day, a year or two after I had begun to work at Elder Home Care, I received a telephone call from a trustee on the nominating committee of the Memorial Hospital board. I was asked if I would be willing to serve on the board. The committee believed that because of my work with older people, I would bring a valuable and necessary perspective. I was overwhelmed. In years past, Memorial Hospital hadn't even employed any Jewish doctors; they all went to work at City Hospital, instead. Moreover, after I accepted, I received a questionnaire that asked about my experiences, including my military service. Clearly, few women had served on this board.

By that point in my career, I had been involved with quite a few non-profit organizations. I knew very well where the locus of power and decision-making was on any board. It took me awhile, but I eventually ended up where I wanted to be, on both the Executive and the Finance Committees. I had three mentors: Russ Fuller, Myles McDonough and George Hazzard, all of whom gave me good counsel and helped me move up the ranks.

George Hazzard, then president of Worcester Polytechnic Institute, was the chairman of the Strategic Planning Committee when I first joined it. He was wonderful to me. He shared important information, and, when he retired, I became chairman in his stead. Of all the things we accomplished on that committee, the one I remember most is the construction of the bridge from the new parking garage into the hospital itself. In 1992, a new Emergency Room was being added to the east side of the hospital. Plans called for a parking garage for visitors to be built on that same side, with a drive for ambulances bisecting the two structures.

When the architect brought the plans for the garage to our

committee, I said, "But there's no direct entrance from the garage into the hospital." A visitor would have had to take the elevator in the garage down to the first floor and then cross the ambulance driveway in order to get into the hospital on the main level.

The architect patiently explained that any other option would ruin the aesthetics of the architectural design.

I said, "Are you telling me that my older folks are going to drop off their spouses at the hospital entrance, go park in the garage, come down the elevator and walk across the ambulance driveway in rain and snow and sleet? Some ambulance will toot its horn and they'll drop dead, right in the driveway. That's not acceptable. If I have to, I will lie down on the ground and refuse to let you build."

Everybody looked at me.

Then, meekly, one after another, they all said, "She's right. You can't do that. You'd better bring in another plan."

Although he didn't want to, the architect devised a new design that included a bridge between the garage and the hospital, crossing over the ambulance driveway at the third floor. From there, visitors could take an elevator down to the hospital lobby.

He wasn't very happy, but I was ecstatic. I have always thought that they should have named that bridge the "Lois B. Green Bridge." Of course, they didn't, but I love it, and I call it "my bridge" to myself. Without my interceding, it would never have been built. I loved doing that. And I do believe, even today, that I was absolutely right. You simply couldn't put the frail, elderly or infirm at risk, especially in bad weather.

In 1992, I became vice chairman of the Memorial board,

and then chairman two years later.

Shortly before I took over as chairman, I was driving to a meeting with Peter Levine, who was the Chief Executive Officer of the hospital. Peter is probably one of my dearest friends. We both have exactly the same Myers-Briggs profile, and we were a real team. We served together on the board of the Massachusetts Hospital Association and spent a lot of time driving to meetings and retreats together. We had a chance to talk through a lot of hospital issues.

He said, "Lois, I have something to say to you. I have a concern about your becoming chairman."

I said, "Well, what's your concern, Peter?"

He said, "My concern is that you've been an executive director, and you're used to management. I'm worried that you're going to overstep your bounds and get involved in day-to-day management."

I said, "Peter, you're absolutely right. I probably will. Not only am I used to it, but it's also my personality. So all you have to do is say, 'Lois, you're overstepping your bounds,' and I'll shut up. I know perfectly well that board members shouldn't get involved in day-to-day operations, but that's not going to stop me. So you stop me."

Adding to the problem was the fact that I was so comfortable at Memorial. I had had all my children there, as well as my treatment for uterine cancer. I knew a lot of the doctors because of my involvement in the hospital. I knew a lot of the social workers because many of them had come from Elder Home Care, where they had been case managers. Whenever I had a doctor's appointment with anyone on staff, the physician would say to me, "You know, this is the problem at Memorial." The person in charge of the kitchen always made me chocolate chip cookies and shared all the hospital gossip with me. People told me things. So I had all this information, and many times I believed I knew something that Peter ought to know. When that was the case, I used to poke my head around the edge of his office door and say, "Can I overstep my bounds?" Of course, after awhile, he said, "Forget about it. Just come in."

When Peter became CEO, he set up the innovative concept of a physician advisory committee, a relatively new idea in the world of hospital administration. It was a non-voting committee with some power, intended to keep physicians informed and to solicit their advice. Peter appointed some members, and the doctors elected the others themselves.

At the beginning, there were no women on the physician advisory board. They had competed against one another, and so no one had received enough votes. A group of women doctors came to me and asked if I would help them learn about boards so that they could gain some representation. They were interested in my help not because I was a trustee, but because I had facilitated board trainings. I asked them if they would come to the meetings if I developed a program for them. They said yes, but of course I wasn't sure whether they were all going to attend. With the help of Cathy Recht, a nurse in administration, we set up a monthly program. Every other month, the session focused on hospital business, managed care, for instance, or how to read a budget. The alternative sessions emphasized issues central to women's lives, such as how to balance work and family. The reality was that many hospital meetings took place in the early morning or late afternoon, just when women doctors were carpooling or trying to take care of their families.

I'm sure they went to the meetings in their own departments. But their personal lives meant that they were missing the opportunity to be part of the running of the hospital.

Ours was to be a nine-month program. Nine months – I thought that was pretty funny. Before we started, I went to Peter Levine and said, "Peter, if I run this program, will you guarantee that the women who finish it will end up on a committee?" He promised, but he said he was a little hurt that I hadn't asked him to participate. So we changed it to ten months, and he spoke to the group at the final session. I made him pay for a dinner at the Worcester Club so that the women could celebrate their hard work. There were ten women who went through the entire program, and the next year I was thrilled to see their names on every important committee.

I loved doing it. In fact, some of the male physicians asked why I hadn't put together such a program for them! I learned a lot from the women physicians. I became friends with a number of them, and they educated me about how difficult it was for them to be treated as equals in the medical profession. It was another opportunity for me to understand how thick the glass ceiling was for women in the workplace.

Near the end of 1996, when I was chairman of the board, we hired a consultant to advise us as we began to discuss the possibility of merging with another hospital. Integrated health care had begun to define medicine at this time, and we weren't sure we could make it on our own in competition with Fallon, St. Vincent's, and the University of Massachusetts clinical system. We examined the pluses and minuses of merging with UMass or with a Boston hospital. I learned a lot about strategic planning and cost benefit analysis.

At the same time, UMass was considering whether, as a medical school, they could afford to keep their clinical system afloat. I remember going to a hush-hush meeting at a hotel in Westborough to discuss whether there was interest in our merging, and how we could do it. As we embarked on more serious negotiations, I was the only woman in the entire process. It was so male-oriented, focused on power and ego and winning and losing. Though I was amused, at the same time I was apprehensive. To me, it seemed that Memorial was a bit naïve as we faced off against this large academic entity. But ultimately, supported by our own consultants and legal team, we did fine. In 1997, we agreed to go forward with the merger.

At a celebratory dinner, I received a Steuben bridge from UMass Medical School that represented how the two organizations were going to join together. I thought it was being given to me as a representative of Memorial, but they said it was just for me, because I had been so involved in making it happen. At the same time, I received the Presidential Award from Memorial, and my picture now hangs in the lobby of what is called the Presidents' Hall. So many people tell me, "I went to the hospital for surgery this morning, and when I saw your picture, it made me feel better." Or, "I saw your picture, and I just knew that my child was going to get better." It has served this very strange purpose of giving people comfort. One day, I was doing a training for United Way, and a young woman came up to me and said, "I'm carrying twins, and one isn't doing well. Every time I go into the hospital, I see your picture, and I know it's going to be all right." I said to her, "Don't do that, because I can't make those things happen." Ultimately, she lost the babies, and I felt this strange sense of responsibility.

Of course, that's just silly, because it's only a picture. But I find that in some way it plays the same role for me. It hangs directly across the hall from the Radiology Department, and every time I am having a CT-scan and scared to death about what the results might be, I look at my picture and smile. My heart has always been at Memorial.

We argued about the details of the merger throughout 1997 and into 1998. Peter Levine, who was an eternal optimist, vowed that it would not be a matter of one institution swallowing another in the long run, but rather A plus B equaling C. I thought it was a view of the world according to Peter, and not very realistic. Indeed, the process was quite complicated. The UMass Medical School would remain a public institution, but the university's clinical system would merge with ours and become a non-profit organization. Some physicians were state employees; others were not; some worked both at the medical school and in the clinics. At every step, for good or for bad, the legislature had to be involved. There was a lot of back and forth and many legal issues to iron out.

That winter, we met at the Chatham Bars Inn on Cape Cod. The group included six or seven from each hospital. I was one of two representative trustees, and my UMass counterpart and I went to the Cape for two days near the end of the retreat. I was the only woman. Again, I felt as though Memorial were playing on an uneven field. Once more, it was a question of who was going to win and who was going to lose, rather than how we could work it out so that there were two winners. In some ways, the negotiations were incredibly childish as well. We would offer a suggestion, and the UMass representatives would say, "We need to caucus about that." And off they would go into another room to talk privately. It might be telling tales out of school, but the Memorial group used to take quarter bets to see how long the caucus would take. If the UMass people walked out at 10 A.M., one of us would take 10:15, someone else 10:18, and so on.

Ultimately, it was decided that Peter Levine would remain the CEO of the combined hospital for three years. Bob Karam, from UMass, would be chairman of the board and I would be vice chairman. After three years, Peter would step down, Art Russo from UMass would take over as CEO, and I would become the new chairman. Unfortunately, we left some sticky issues to be resolved later, and they never were. The situation led to enormous tension between the two institutions as well as between Peter Levine and Aaron Lazare, the chancellor of the Medical School.

My three years as vice chairman of this combined board were interesting ones. There were ten trustees from Memorial, five from the Medical School, including one student, and five from the University of Massachusetts. I was the trustee liaison to the Children's Medical Center and also the only trustee on the hospital quality improvement committee. Our board was focused primarily on finance. At the very end of a meeting, we might spend some time discussing issues having to do with the quality of patient care. I was much more interested in those topics and felt that they should be given greater priority by the board. So I was very much looking forward to making some changes when I became chairman.

In August of 2000, the summer before I was to take over in June, a vote came before the board to consider whether the vice chairman automatically moved up to the chairmanship. I asked what such a proposal might mean, and the answer was that it would make the by-laws more adaptable. I ran the meeting that day because Bob Karam couldn't be there, and I remember saying, as a joke, "Well, I suppose I'll have to politic in order to get my position." Everyone laughed.

But the vote didn't sit well with me, and over the course of the next six months, I asked everybody I knew whether the real intention was to block me from becoming chairman. They all said I was being ridiculous, and of course I was going to be chairman. Finally, one or two inside people took me aside and told me, "Lois, they're planning to get rid of you." And I said, "Well, why haven't they told me?"

The year progressed, and I continued to be the kind of trustee who consistently asked the tough questions. At one point, there was a discussion about UMass Medical School's setting up a subsidiary of the hospital. I leaned across the table just as everyone was about to vote and asked, "Why would we want to do that?" And it turned out that we never did it because it wasn't quite kosher.

In April that year, I was diagnosed with breast cancer and had surgery. In May, Bob was diagnosed with terminal lung cancer. We were sitting at home one afternoon after I had had my first chemo treatment, and Art Russo came over. He had taken over as CEO because Peter Levine had been ill. Art came into my house and sat on the porch and told me that they did not want me to be chairman of the board. They had already asked Sumner "Tony" Tilton, a local attorney who happened also to be Bob's and my personal lawyer, and he had agreed to take over. Art told me that I could remain on the board, but I would not be on the executive, finance or strategic planning committees.

I was absolutely stunned. When he left, I cried and cried. I think I cried for months. Indeed, even all these years later my eyes fill up just thinking about it. I couldn't believe that anybody would actually treat me that way. Moreover, only two people on the board had defended me, and only one, Dennis Dmitri, had spoken up. Dennis was a physician in the community and was very upset. The way they had done it was so cruel. Given my illness, I had already wondered whether it was wise to take on the chairmanship while I was going through chemotherapy. I had thought perhaps that someone else could fill in for me for a year. But I had never expected to be treated this way.

I went to the meeting of the nominating committee, where Tony Tilton was officially nominated, and then I came home and wrote a letter of resignation. I assured Tony that I "do not disagree with the outcome" but rather that "my unhappiness has been with the process." I resigned not only my board position but also its attendant responsibilities – board liaison to the Children's Medical Center, member of the Quality Improvement Committee and member of both the Massachusetts Hospital Association Board and the American Hospital Association Committee on Governance. (The AHA Committee asked me to finish my term. I had loved that committee, made up of hospital trustees who come together from all over the country. I will be forever grateful that they allowed me to stay.) It was, I wrote, "a very sad day for me" as I gave up "all the things I love and enjoy ... I don't believe I had another choice." In the end, I wrote, "After 18 years of service to both Memorial and UMMHC, I believe I deserved better treatment."

Not long after, I received a call from a reporter at the Telegram & Gazette, asking me what had happened. I had no intention of undercutting the hospital, which was already having financial difficulties, or of undermining my own dignity. I quelled the rumor that I had resigned in protest against major cutbacks of staff and departments and, in fact, noted that I supported the "very tough decisions that have to be made." I had, I said, stepped down for personal reasons. I wished Tony Tilton well and noted only that "my eyes filled with tears when I left."

After the article came out, Art Russo called me and thanked me for "being a lady" and for not divulging what had actually occurred. They knew very well how badly they had treated me. Art Russo resigned as CEO only two months later, but still no one asked me to come back onto the board. As I look back at my entire life, I cannot think of another time when anything hurt me as much as this episode.

But I will always love Memorial Hospital. I never wanted to punish the hospital for what had been done to me personally by a handful of individuals. I still believe that it is a marvelous institution, giving wonderful care. It is my hospital, and it is taking care of me as I near the end of my life.

Ironically, shortly after the board debacle, I received a call from Patricia Droney at UMass Medical School. As part of a two-year public health course on "Physician, Patient and Society," first year medical students at UMass select a two-week clerkship in the community on one of twenty or so topics, including health policy, the underserved, women's health etc. Patricia asked me to direct the geriatric clerkship, which would introduce students to different aspects of elder care. I declined, telling her that my husband was terminally ill and that I was finishing chemotherapy and about to start a course of radiation.

I did agree to give her some advice, and so I sat with her in the cafeteria of the medical school one afternoon and talked to her about the community agencies that served elders. I told her exactly whom to call in each agency and helped her think about ideal placements for students. She asked then if I would be willing to speak to the students.

That fall, when the program started, Bob had just died, and I was in the middle of radiation. However, I agreed to meet with the students to share with them what it was like to live in the community as an older person. I told them that fully 95% of all older people would probably prefer to remain in their own homes rather than go into a nursing home. When they became physicians, I hoped that they would turn to services and programs in the community that facilitated at-home care rather than automatically sending their patients to nursing homes.

A few months later, I spoke about the loss of my husband and end-of-life issues to another group of UMass medical students who were taking a course called "The Spirituality of Dying." The following spring, once again I was asked to take over the geriatric clerkship, and this time I said yes.

And so, a year after I had in effect been dumped from the board of UMMHC, it was with great self-satisfaction that I found myself listed as a faculty member at the Medical School, approved by the Family Practice group as an instructor. I spent the summer of 2002 developing a program for the students and ran it for the first time that fall. I have done so ever since. About three years ago, students in the graduate school of nursing joined the course, and my group now blends medical students and graduate nursing students.

It is a very structured clerkship, and I believe that they

learn a great deal. I try to keep them engaged and involved; I don't believe that they should sit and be lectured to. They visit a different agency every day, meeting with experts on a full range of topics. At the Senior Center, they see programs focusing on wellness. They spend a day with Protective Services at Elder Services, learning about the program and visiting with people who are either being abused or suffering from self-neglect. They attend a team meeting at the Summit, a full spectrum day program for older people who must be eligible for nursing home placement in a protective environment.

At UMass Memorial Home Health, they attend to a hospice team meeting to hear a range of experts discuss individual cases. The students then visit homes with hospice nurses. At Jewish Family Service, they learn about the guardianship program, set up for older people who cannot take care of themselves or their finances and have no family members to step forward. On another day, they go to the New England Dream Center, a social day care center where the participants do not need medical care, but many have some kind of mental impairment. I deliberately choose a day when there are no volunteers present, so the students have to pitch in. Naturally, as a Jewish mother, I was concerned about feeding them. When I took over the program, they complained that they had to go from one place to another during the day, and they never knew where to eat. So I worked it out that every agency they visit has to give them lunch.

On the very last morning, each of them shadows a different geriatrician in his or her practice. Then, in the afternoon, they come to my house for lunch. Students in every clerkship work together on a group project and evaluation, which culminates in a poster show. After lunch, they spread themselves out in my loft with their slides and pictures and computers and work on their poster.

I am both the faculty member and their preceptor; I am with them all the time, except when they are out visiting clients or patients with nurses or social workers. They ask all sorts of questions, and because of my experience and knowledge of older people in the community, I can answer most of them. Moreover, I had overseen the care of my mother and taken care of Bob for four months while he was dying. And, of course, I am a patient myself. In reality, I know the whole continuum of care, from the least to the most restrictive. I believe that perspective has been very helpful to my students. I always tell them, "You're the luckiest of all the groups. In Corrections, they don't have a prisoner as their faculty member, and in Long-term Hospital Care, they don't have a patient, but here you have a real live geriatric teaching you."

The students are required to keep a journal about their experiences, and from the very start I told them I didn't want to read about where they went and what they did. I was with them all the time; I knew exactly what their schedule was. Instead, I wanted them to tell me how they felt and what they had learned. The journals have been absolutely wonderful. I remember so many of the comments. Several years ago, speaking about the clerkship to the American Association of Medical Colleges, I quoted from some of the entries. One student wrote that "Case managers have no relation to their clients but I wouldn't have known that from watching them work... It has increased my drive to be the best doctor I can be." Another "had an a priori vision of a homogeneous senior population with a fixed set of needs... Over the course of this clerkship, these assumptions were proved superficial, and I realized that the depth and breadth of issues and available services exceeded my expectations."

At times, reading my students' journals helps me understand the issues that they themselves are grappling with. One year, I had a student who didn't seem to be actively engaged. She was so ill at ease that I worried the clerkship wasn't the right one for her. Her first journal entry admitted that "I am terrified of aging. I don't ever want to grow old and have to deal with the health problems, logistical issues of healthcare, and heartache of seeing my friends and family pass away. I don't want to become 'helpless' and have to rely on others to help me with everyday tasks. I can't even being to imagine how difficult it is for some of these seniors to have lived such long and productive independent lives and then get to a point where they must admit (or worse, be told) they are no longer capable of caring for themselves." At the end of the clerkship, she wrote that she believed she was going to be a very good physician as a result of her experience.

One year, at one of the agencies, the students participated in an exercise meant to mimic the process of loss that so often comes with growing older. They had to write down the ten things that meant the most to them in life and then give them up, one by one, by putting the slips of paper in a basket in order of least to most important. It had a profound impact on them. Indeed, some found it so painful that they couldn't get through the whole exercise. One wrote, "I had to hold back tears thinking of losing my brother and sister, my parents, my freedom and physical capacities. I was only pretending to lose these things, and I can not even imagine what it is like to really lose them."

For me, playing a role in influencing health professionals to begin to understand the whole patient has been deeply important. In a hospital setting, older people are often bewildered. Think about it: you go into the hospital, they take away your hearing aids, they take away your glasses, you're in bed, you're in a strange place. There are a lot of studies now being done on delirium among older patients who are so disoriented that they don't know where they are. Medical and nursing students work with them, but patients go home so quickly now that the students aren't able to see their progress. The geriatric clerkship gives students a different perspective. They are able to interact with chronically ill older people who maintain their sense of humor and function in the community, despite memory loss or other issues. Indeed, in recent years, changes in the third and fourth year curricula at the medical school have begun to incorporate more experience with geriatrics, both in and outside of the hospital setting. Such exposure is key not only for internists, but for a range of other specialties as well. Third year medical students now do an internship on end-of-life issues.

For the first few years, when I sat with my students on the first day and asked each of them why they had chosen geriatrics, the response was varied. Some said, "They put me in this one," or "I have a grandmother." Last fall, however, everyone around the table was there because they wanted to be there.

My students have watched me as I struggle to deal with the impact of my own illness. In 2008, I was in bad shape from the chemotherapy, although I continued to be with the students every day. They treated me with such care, helping me down stairs and to do things. I shared a lot with them, and it helped me to talk with them about end-of-life issues as well as my own wishes. I have cautioned them that, although they spend four years learning how to save lives, they need to understand the importance of allowing people to die with dignity in the setting of their choice. I think that in me they see an active, contented, busy older person who is facing the end of life, and I hope that it gives them both insight and some balance.

It is critical for end-of-life issues to be taught in medical school. Young people have such trouble confronting their own mortality. I believe that so many people end their lives attached to tubes and machines against their wishes because physicians find it so difficult to let patients know that they don't have long to live. If doctors were educated to discuss end-of-life plans with their younger, healthy patients during regular checkups, then it might be possible to avoid the painful deliberations that come when patients are already nearing death. Incorporating the teaching of such practices in medical education would bring about tremendous change in the way we approach the end of life. I have urged my own students to think about letting someone die when it was time, without heroic measures to save them; to be able to talk about the choices; to listen to the concerns of patients and their families; to support their wishes. I want them to acknowledge their own fears, so they can communicate with their patients with compassion and understanding.

The clerkship has been a marvelous experience in so many ways. As much as the students appreciate and love it, the community agencies, too, are delighted to be involved and to share what they know. They invest time and energy in providing the students with the best possible introduction they can, arranging visits, mentors and presentations. The community effort is wonderful. Every spring, we have a thank-you breakfast and invite everyone who has participated.

For my part, I treat the clerkship not as volunteer work, but as a paid position. (I think I am the only unpaid faculty member. The others who give their time do it in the course of their regular jobs. I complain bitterly at every opportunity, but in all these years no one has paid the slightest attention to me!) I spend a great deal of time preparing, as well as reading and grading the journals. I always tell the students that I am a very tough grader. What I don't tell them is that I hover sometimes between an A and an A minus. I love it. The teaching of these students has been a reward in and of itself. I continue to hear from them, sometimes years afterward. Not long ago, I had dinner at the Flying Rhino with one of my graduate nurses, now out of school and working. It gives me such pleasure to know that I have made a difference in their lives.

Several years ago, I received an honorary degree from the medical school for my work with the clerkship, though it was also probably related to my involvement with the merger and elder care in the community. I think it might have been in lieu of pay! I spoke at graduation, which was held in Mechanics Hall. I was, I told them, very pleased to get the honor, but I was a little disappointed because I had been hoping to get a medical degree. After all, I had been practicing medicine without a license for fifty years! I didn't speak long; they were at their own graduation, and didn't need to hear a longwinded speech. I left them with three short messages: to commit themselves to ensuring the right of everyone to quality affordable health care; to stand up for what they believed in, emphasizing honesty and integrity; and, to "take good care of us old folk."

"Keep us in our homes as long as possible with dignity and respect," I said, "and when it's time for us to die (with apologies to Dylan Thomas), DO let us go gentle into that good night."

Finally, I offered them one of my favorite sayings, a Native American proverb: "On the day you were born, you cried and the world rejoiced. Live your life so that on the day you die, the world will cry and you will rejoice."

To Have Succeeded

To laugh often and love much:
To win respect of intelligent people
And the affection of children;
To earn the approbation of honest critics
And endure the betrayal of false friends;
To appreciate beauty;
To find the best in others;
To give one's self;
To leave the world a little better,
Whether by a healthy child,
A garden patch,
Or redeemed social condition;
To have played and laughed with enthusiasm
And sung with exultation;
To know even one life has breathed easier
Because you have lived ...
This is to have succeeded.
-Ralph Waldo Emerson

CHAPTER EIGHT

THAT FAT LITTLE GIRL IS STILL DEEP INSIDE ME

I n 1993, in a marvelous "star for a night" celebration, I
received the Isaiah Thomas Award from the Advertising
Club of Worcester. Named for one of Worcester's first citizens,
the Isaiah Thomas Award is the most prestigious honor that a
volunteer can receive in the city. It is now under the jurisdiction
of the Worcester *Telegram & Gazette* and conferred as one
of the newspaper's several Visions Community Awards. But
when I received the award, the evening focused only on the
single recipient. In all of the years I had been attending this
event in honor of other people, the program had always been
very serious and the speakers erudite. I was determined to put
together a different kind of night. I chose my husband as master
of ceremonies, and I asked my two closest friends, Barbara
Greenberg and Joan Sadowsky, to be the keynote speakers. My

rabbi, Jim Simon from Temple Emanuel, gave the invocation, and Father George Reuger, whom I had known from Elder Home Care days, gave the benediction.

It was the most stupendous moment of my entire life: the culmination of all my work in the community. Much of my family was there – my mother, my sister and brother, my children. Many of my friends came. If I remember correctly, there were over 400 people gathered in Mechanics Hall that evening.

Bob was wonderful, funny and warm, cracking jokes while at the same time making it clear just how proud he was of me. At one point, he noted, "Lois gives unselfishly of her time, her energy, and our resources," commenting that I attended "more meetings per pound than anyone else in the country." I was, he said, envious of only one other woman in the world, and that was Prime Minister Golda Meir, "because she got to run a whole country." Jeff Mulford, the city manager of Worcester, and city councilor John Anderson both spoke about my involvement in and commitment to the Worcester community. There were endless jokes from everyone – with the possible exception of Rabbi Simon and Father Reuger -- about how I loved to boss and take charge!

When Barbara and Joan spoke, they each stood at different lecterns and traded memories of our early years together, a reflection of a different time when we left our doors unlocked and the quality of life was markedly more tranquil. They spoke about the importance of voluntarism and making a difference, noting that it was more important "now more than ever to take our responsibility seriously." To finish, they introduced a beautiful slide show, produced by Joe Pagano. With "To

Succeed," my favorite passage from Ralph Waldo Emerson as a backdrop, photographs showed me at work and Worcester as a vibrant community.

Once in awhile, I watch the DVD recording we had made of the evening, and read the booklet that was given to everyone. And I still can't believe that it all actually happened to me, a woman and Jewish!

That sense of disbelief has continued to haunt me throughout my life, no matter how successful I have been. There are so many plaques and certificates framed on my study wall that I cannot hang them all. I have honorary degrees from every institution with which I have been involved, from the University of Massachusetts Medical School to Becker College to Clark University. I have been asked to speak countless times, at an infinite number of organizations, meetings and assemblies. People ask me for advice all the time, both professionally and informally.

And yet, every time something good happens to me, I am not only astonished, but I cannot quite believe that they have the right person. How could anyone possibly think that the fat little girl from Hartford, the one whose mother never liked her, deserves such attention? I feel like an imposter, certain that someone is about to knock on my door and finger me as the fraud I sometimes believe I am. I've come to learn that such feelings are not unusual among women, even those of us who have been lucky enough not only to meet some of our goals but also to receive recognition for them. Yet, in my case, I know that the root of my insecurity – oddly paired with what can only be described as a consummate self-confidence – lies in my childhood and my relationship with my mother. That little girl who still lives inside of me has to keep pinching herself. I don't ever take anything for granted. Instead, I always marvel to myself, "Can you imagine that someone thinks I'm good enough to do this?" I know I'm good enough, just as I knew I was responsible when I was young and Fran trusted me to take care of Judy. But I have never quite believed that anyone else thought I was good enough.

Although many of the anxieties that plagued me as a child have dissipated, I still retain a few of them. For example, just as Joel and I couldn't bear to be late when we were young for fear we would miss something, I still always have to be early. Bob was wonderful about it. When we were traveling, he would ask, "Okay, what time do you want to get to the airport?" If we had to sit for two hours before we could board the plane, he wouldn't say a word, though he might glower at me. He knew that getting there much too early was the only way I could deal with my anxiety about being late. When I first used to go to meetings after I came to Worcester, I was always the first person there. It was annoying to be there on time and wait; nobody else was ever on time. So I tried to train myself. I would make myself stop at the grocery store first. But I would still get to the meeting early, and stopping at the grocery store made me so anxious that I gave up. Instead, I brought a book, and I sat there reading until everyone else showed up. That's still the way I am. I feel knots in my stomach if I'm running late. Wherever I am going, I have to leave early to make sure I arrive on time.

There are other remnants of my difficult childhood. I still have to read the end of a book before I start at the beginning; I also ask about the ending of a movie before I see it. No matter what might be going on in my life, I always climb into bed and go right to sleep. If there is a real crisis, I might wake up suddenly at 4:30 in the morning. But most of the time, I can lie there and think about other things, a book or a movie, calming myself down. I learned as a child that the world doesn't ever look as bleak in the morning.

One of the most lasting impacts of my mother's influence has to do with my attitude toward food and my weight. I've never been able to shake my anxiety about being fat. After I had Sarah, and I was even more concerned about how much I weighed, my doctor gave me Preludin as an appetite suppressant. It was fairly commonly used in the 1950s, and I had no idea that it was speed. I soon found that taking a pill in the morning wasn't enough, so I took one at noon, too. I was really thin. I weighed 120 pounds, and I was very happy; I was a size six. Then one day I found myself taking a third pill at four o'clock in the afternoon. I threw the contents of the bottle down the toilet.

Even now, although I am living with a bad diagnosis, I continue to get on the scale three or four times a day, sometimes with my sneakers on, because I know what I weigh with my sneakers on. I eat no potatoes, no white rice, no sour cream and no white bread. I've learned that if I eat lobster, or something that is salty, I will have gained two pounds in the morning, and then I will lose it. The few times I've been in the hospital, I haven't eaten the potato or the bread. I'm very careful. When I make dinner by myself, I make a piece of chicken and fresh or frozen vegetables. I will never take a medication if one of the side effects is weight gain. In 2001, I was so sick from the chemo treatments, and the doctor wanted to give me marijuana pills. But, she told me, you'll gain some weight. So I threw them away.

I love chocolate, so I allow myself one Hershey nugget a day. That's my sweet. But if I have a whole Hershey bar, I'll take one bite and throw the rest in the trash so I can't finish it. I treat myself once in a blue moon to ice cream, which I adore. When I was dieting in college because I wanted to lose weight before our wedding, I ate nothing on Sundays and then went out and had ice cream. Years later, when my dear friend Barbara's husband, Leo Rudnick, died suddenly, Rabbi Klein called me to let me know. I said to him, "Rabbi Klein, you're lying. Leo is only 50 years old. I'm ashamed of you, being a rabbi." I hung up on him. Bob was in Florida, and I was picking him up at the airport. I went right out and bought a huge dish of ice cream, which is what I did when I was happy or sad or upset. Food was my comfort as a child, and it still is.

When the children were small, Bob and I had a deal. Bob loved junk candy, Tootsie Rolls, all that stuff. I said to him, "I can't control my love of sweets. You can bring anything home from the grocery store that you want as long as it's not chocolate." He was wonderful. He used to say to me, "You don't have to keep doing this. I fell in love with you when you were heavy." I'd look at these sylph-like models and say to him, "Aren't they gorgeous?" And he would say, "Oh, no, they're too bony. They're awful." Even after all of those years, I still couldn't believe that he could love me fat.

I am well aware that weight is an issue for me. I know it's outrageous to get on a scale three or four times a day. Even when you're dieting, they tell you to weigh yourself only once a week. My children discuss my attitude toward food. Patty thinks it's the saddest thing in the world. She says to me, "you don't even enjoy it, because if you treat yourself, you feel guilty." She won't talk to me about it or pay any attention to what or how much I'm eating. She tells everyone who eats with me that the rule at the table is that no one can discuss food with me. The threads that run through my life – my anxieties, my concern about my weight, my wanting to be loved, my coping skills – all began in childhood.

For years, I had a recurring dream. In the dream, I am at the beach with my children, and Bob is in Worcester. Something terrible is about to happen: a tidal wave, a hurricane, a tornado. I have to bundle up the kids and get out of there before it hits. But first, as I had done every year since I was a child at the beach with my grandmother, I have to close up the cottage. There is no one to help me. The kids are too little. While they are playing outside, I empty the refrigerator, wrapping all of the shelves in newspaper so they won't rust, and do the same with the stove. I wash all the sheets and cover the beds with bedspreads. I take down the porch screens and store them in the living room, bring in the outside furniture, etc. As I go through this routine, I am getting more panicked as the disaster approaches. I always wake up before the storm hits us. It is always the same dream, but the nature of the calamity changes. For some reason, it never occurs to me that the cottage will be wiped away, and so the sensible thing to do would be to put the children in the car and flee. After many years, the dream stopped. Then, a few weeks ago, I had it again.

I will never know the dream's meaning unless I have it interpreted. Is it a nightmare? Perhaps. Or maybe I was afraid of my mother's wrath if I didn't close up the cottage perfectly. As a child, I had certainly been made aware of the consequences of not following the rules. Even without much analysis, it seems clear that my mother's influence continued to pervade my life, even after Bob and I married and I left Hartford.

She hadn't liked Bob at first, though she came to love him. When I first brought him home, in addition to wondering how he could love me when I was fat, she also told me that I should have fallen in love with a rich man. Bob thought giving $25 to Federation was a big deal. Even that was far more than he could really afford at the time. Our family was so charitable that she held him to the same standard, not bothering to consider that he had very little money. After Bob and I were married and we moved to Worcester, I avoided going to Hartford, knowing that I had to put some distance between my mother and me. Bob himself had been very clear about that. I was so attached to my cousins and my family that, when I was still at Bryn Mawr, I had urged him to look for a job in Hartford. He said, "Lois, if we lived in Hartford, our marriage wouldn't last a year."

My mother came back into my life on a regular basis after I had Sarah. She came to Worcester to take care of her when she was born, and often babysat. They adored each other. In fact, she probably knew Sarah best of all of the grandchildren. They all loved her. She was tough, but she was good to them. I remember once being in Hartford with Sarah, who couldn't have been more than two. We went to the grocery store, and my mother told her could pick out a candy bar to eat after lunch. On the way home in the car, Sarah started to eat the candy, and my mother took it away from her and threw it out of the window because she had broken the deal. My mother had always treated me exactly the same way. When I was studying for my finals at Bryn Mawr, right before we were married, I remember coming down the stairs at home with a cigarette in my mouth. My mother said to me then, "If you give up smoking, I'll buy you a washer and dryer." Bob and I had no money, so that was a very tempting offer. "When do I get it?" I asked. And my mother said, "If you can go through exams and the wedding without smoking, then I'll get it for you then." So I quit. Two or three years later, I started smoking again, and Sarah, who was only 2 ½, told on me. My mother made me give her the money back. That's the kind of person she was. She made a deal, I broke the deal, and I had to pay her back $500. My children never minded her strictness. They just took her for what she was. The day she took the candy away from Sarah, Sarah cried all the way home, but she never blamed my mother. Indeed, Sarah could never understand how I felt about my mother. My cousins thought she was wonderful, too. They all loved Aunt Adeline.

After I had children, my mother was always in and out of my life. We spent every summer together at the cottage at the beach, and so they grew up with her. Even so, I never forgot the time when I was small when I refused to eat squash at lunch and had to confront it on my plate again that night at dinner. If there was an issue when I was an adult, I probably either laughed or sloughed it off. She and Aunt Min used to come to our little apartment in Worcester and rearrange all the furniture. I never said anything to them. I just put it all back after they left. She often lectured me because Patty and Rachel, two years apart, would only come to her house together. They were inseparable. My mother thought that was terrible. She thought I should separate them by sending one down to Connecticut at a time. They refused. And here they are, years later, at ages 47 and 49, talking to each other on the telephone every single day. I grew braver as I got older. My mother always complained about my brother's wife. I remember saying to her, "Mom, I am not going to be part of a triangle."

Once, Senator Abraham Ribicoff came to speak to the Brotherhood at Temple Emanuel, and Bob picked him up in Hartford. We knew him because he was my Uncle Sam's and Uncle Eddie's best friend. Afterward, Bob and I drove him to Logan Airport together. We were talking about something, and the Senator turned around and said to me, "Gee, you're really smart. I thought your sister was the only smart one." Clearly, this information had come directly from my mother.

My mother suffered from bipolar disease, as did my sister, though I never knew about Jean until she told me when we were adults. Looking back, I suspect that some of my mother's behavior when I was younger was clearly manic. She often went on buying sprees, and she moved so quickly that I couldn't keep up with her. At times, she suffered from severe depression. The first time I really noticed it was when I was married and went down to Hartford one day to have lunch with her. She wouldn't talk to me. She sat and made odd gestures with her hands, and then she went into the bathroom and stayed there so she didn't have to talk to me. I remember telling my stepfather that she was sick and that he had to do something about it. At some point, she had shock treatments for the depression. Once when she went to Hartford Hospital to be treated, she told me that she had taken my telephone number with her because she had been told that shock therapy adversely affected the memory. She called later to tell me that she had remembered my number on her own after all. She had to have several rounds of shock treatment, but eventually ended up taking Lithium, which seemed to keep her fairly stable.

When I went through menopause, I was concerned about not being able to have hormonal replacement therapy because of my history of cancer. I thought the family history of depression might catch up with me. But I never had to deal with depression. Mental illness bypassed me, as did the terrible migraines that afflicted both my mother and my sister. At the end of my mother's life, her psychiatrist told me that he thought narcissistic personality disorder was probably a more accurate diagnosis for her than bipolar disease. Certainly, she was narcissistic. When my son, David, and his wife, Wendy, lost Eli, their first child who died from Canavan's Disease, my mother said to them, "How could God do this to me?"

I am sure that she did many things that bothered me as we both grew older, but I haven't retained a memory of any incident that seemed particularly distressing. At the end, however, as she grew frail and old, things came almost full circle for me. It was at that point that I began to confront my relationship with my mother, and to think about the way she had treated me as a child, and since.

In the early 1980s, I helped my mother and stepfather move into a condominium in Simsbury, near West Hartford. I went to their house every day to pack up for them before the movers arrived. The playroom where my mother had punished Joel and me with the belt was filled with boxes. My mother loved to collect things, virtually to the point of hoarding. As I began to go through the boxes, I discovered 100 Revlon compacts, gilded, with fake jewels on top. They were hideous. I said to her, "Mom, we're going to give these away." She said, "How could you? Somebody may want them." A version of this conversation went on for five days. I arrived at nine o'clock every morning, and she sat in the living room, refusing to let me throw anything out. I found cartons of menus from every cruise she and Harry had ever taken, every dinner they had attended. I went into the storeroom, and there were 100 vases. I would say, "Mom, you can't take all this to a little condo." And she would cry, "You're throwing out my whole life!"

I was running Elder Home Care at the time, and I understood very well how traumatic it was for an older person to leave home after many years. But she was incredibly difficult. As I tried to sort through everything, making piles for the thrift shop, Goodwill, the children, and this and that, I began to boss my stepfather around. I yelled at him! I said, "Do something useful!" And this meek little lamb said, "Okay." I sent him on errands, I sent him out to pick up lunch. After some 40 odd years, I finally opened my mouth to him. What great power! I loved it.

But I wasn't quite as strong in standing up to my mother. When she wept to me, "You're not giving away Grandma's soup pot, are you?" I would take the big dented aluminum pot and put it in the back of my station wagon. Every day, I filled up the back, drove home to Rutland Terrace, walked in the house and said, "Bob, please empty the trunk of the car. Do not say a word. Just put it all in the cellar." I didn't throw any of it out until after she died. I was always certain she would come to Worcester and ask me where those things were. She never did, of course. But I was so afraid of her that when Bob said, "Let's just get rid of that!" I would say, "No, I can't. If she asks me to show her the aluminum pot, it has to be there."

In 1987, my stepfather became ill. He had a hematoma and was in the University of Connecticut Hospital. I went racing down to the hospital and sat by his bed while he talked to me about finances. While he was in surgery, I took my mother to the bank, where we made all the arrangements to add me to their account. By the time we returned to the hospital, Harry had come out of his surgery. He was suddenly both demented and aggressive. During the few days he was hospitalized, I was the one who did certain things to care for him. My mother was so embarrassed she couldn't even watch.

Here I was, the head of an agency providing in-home services for frail, low-income older people, and I couldn't even get my stepfather placed in a decent nursing home. The hospital wanted to send him to a variety of places that were simply unacceptable. Finally, I found one in Simsbury, where they lived, that agreed to take him if I provided aides around the clock for him. We did, but he carried on so that they dumped him back at the hospital and refused to take him back. Yet another call came in the middle of the night to send me flying back to Hartford. It was incredibly difficult for me to cope with all of this. But I'm an organizer; I'm used to being the responsible person. So I met with the hospital personnel and, through a contact, found another nursing home for him, with aides. My mother hated it. She thought they weren't nice enough to him, but in truth, they were wonderful for even taking him. It was a very difficult situation.

I had his health proxy, and I had notified the doctor to come to the nursing home and sign a Do Not Resuscitate Order. About a month after Harry had been at the nursing home, my brother tracked me down at a conference in Hartford to tell me that our stepfather had pneumonia and that the nursing home staff was going to send him to the hospital. "But we have a DNR order,"

I said. And Joel said, "Well, it seems the doctor never got out there to sign it." I said, "Joel, I'm leaving the meeting right now. Do not let them take him to the hospital until I get there." I called the doctor, and he said, "Oh, yeah, I just never got there." So I said, "You call the nursing home, and you tell them not to send him to the hospital."

Then after I hung up, I said to myself, "Who am I to take someone's life? Who do I think I am?" Every family in this situation must have to confront these questions. I called my friend, Jim Fanale, who is a geriatrician in Worcester. He said, "Lois, you're doing the right thing. The kindest thing that could happen to someone is pneumonia, because it is a quiet and peaceful death." So I climbed into the car and raced through Hartford to West Hartford, where Joel met me in the parking lot of the nursing home. Harry had already died.

The day of his funeral, I put my mother in the car and drove her to an assisted living facility that was in the process of being built. It was part of St. Joseph's College, right past Beach Park School and only a block from her old house. It was familiar, and she agreed to move right then and there. We made all the arrangements, and I moved her in sometime in the spring of 1988. She was 82 years old. Nuns ran it, and it was just wonderful. My mother said, "Oh, it's going to be a good place because the nuns will take care of us." When you first brought someone to move in, you were allowed to spend the night. So, on the first evening she was there, I had dinner with my mother and slept in a guest room that night. The next morning, I saw the social worker in charge of the residents. I burst into tears and said, "Who is my mother going to have dinner with tonight? She doesn't know anybody." And the Sister said, "Don't worry, people take care of the new residents."

My mother was there for the next twelve years. I went back and forth to see her. Every time I got behind the wheel in Worcester, I was furious by the time I reached Hartford. Here I was, constantly driving to Hartford to take care of her, leaving my job in the middle of the day, even though she had been so harsh with me when I was young. I finally went to see a therapist. She gave me wonderful advice. She said, "You'll never make your mother into the mother you wish you had had." It was very helpful to me.

Often when I was leaving to return to Worcester, my mother would say, "When are you coming back?" I would tell her, and she would say, "Not until then?" I had that same cloying, frustrating feeling. As I drove home, I would be so tired, completely spent from the energy I had expended as well the anger. Finally, I found a Roy Rogers right at the Connecticut-Massachusetts border on Route 84 that sold soft serve chocolate ice cream. I stopped every time, right there, and had my chocolate ice cream, which comforted me and gave me the energy to get home.

Ten years later, in 1998, my mother was diagnosed with congestive heart failure. Doctors also told us that she had Alzheimer's, which I never quite believed. She always dressed appropriately, she loved her beads, and she went down to the dining room perfectly put together. But she did have some dementia. I used to take her to the psychiatrist, because the Lithium she took for her bipolar disorder had to be monitored. I loved sitting there with her. They would ask her, "Who is the president?" And she would say, "Don't you know?" Or they would ask her what season it was, and she would answer, "What is the matter with you people?" We would get to the car, and she would ask me, "Was that bad?" I would say, "Mom, I loved it. I thought it was wonderful, and they shouldn't be giving you that test any more." Finally, I told the doctor that that was enough. At the age of 93, she no longer needed to be quizzed.

She now had aides all the time. One day after an appointment, we stopped in her little coffee shop, and I went next door to the health office to pick up her medicine. I could hear her talking to the aide. "You know," she said, "I never liked her. And she's so good to me now." She was talking about me. I walked back and said, "Mom, you don't have to tell the aide that." She said, "You couldn't have heard me. You were too far away." Of course, she had no idea that people who don't hear well typically talk loudly.

Shortly after that incident, her psychiatrist called me and said, "Your mother wants to tell you she's sorry. Can you forgive her?" I said, "I suppose I can forgive her, but I'm never going to forget." Actually, I wasn't sure I could even forgive her, but that was what I said. So I picked her up, and we went together to the psychiatrist's office. My mother sat in his chair, behind his desk, because she liked it better. He had to sit in another chair. So, first he sent her out of the room, which annoyed her to no end. He said, "Your mother wants to tell you she's sorry. Will you try?" I said, "Yes, I will try." And I thought to myself, how nice that we're going to close the circle.

She came back in, sat down again in his chair, and faced him. Not me. To him, she said, "I'm sorry for what I've done to you."

I said, "Mom, do you know what love is?"

"Yes," she answered. "My grandchildren love me. I buy

them things."

"Love isn't about money," I told her.

"Well, what is love?" she asked.

I thought this was pretty sad. "Love is being nice to Diane, Joel's wife, whom you don't like, because you love Joel."

She said, "I can't do that."

We ended the conversation. I said, "Come on, I'll take you out to lunch." We had been going to the Tumble Brook Country Club for almost ten years. My mother ordered the same thing every time: center cut tongue on rye bread, thick. She used to stand over them at the deli counter while they made it for her. This time, we arrived at the country club, and she said, "I'll have whatever you're having." I knew that was her funny way of trying to make amends.

I said, "Mom, you know you don't like the salad bar. You never eat it."

"I want to eat what you're eating."

So I made a plate for her and a plate for me, and we sat down at the table. (We always sat at the same table, every time.) She started to poke at the salad.

I said, "Mom, would you like me to go get you a tongue sandwich?"

She said yes.

As I stood up, she looked up at me and said, "Is that what love is?"

In truth, my mother didn't know how to love. When I was going to a therapist myself, trying to figure out how to care for her in these later years when I resented her so, my children told me to ask the doctor how I could be such a loving mother myself without having had a good role model. But I had role models who taught me about love. I had my grandmother, my brother, Annie, Fran. The sad thing was that my mother apparently never understood it.

Two years before she actually died, the congestive heart failure worsened, and we thought she was dying. Bob was in Florida, and I called him and told him he had better come home. When I spoke to him after he arrived in Worcester, he was in a lot of pain. He couldn't eat. I left my mother, and I raced home to see what was going on. He said he would call the doctor in the morning. I called Peter Levine, my friend who was CEO of Memorial Hospital – I was then chairman of the board. I had to tell Peter that I wasn't going to a special retreat meeting we had scheduled. I said, "My mother is sick, and something is wrong with Bob. I don't know what's the matter with him." Peter said, "I'll be right over."

He went upstairs to see Bob, pressed on his stomach, and Bob yelled. He had a pain threshold that was set at about 1000. He never complained about pain. Peter said, "It's not his appendix. There's something wrong with his gall bladder. He's going to the hospital right now." Bob said, "I'll go in the morning." Peter said, "You're going right now." So I took him to the hospital, and it turned out that he had a gangrenous gall bladder. He would have died of sepsis. He was sick for a very long time.

In the meantime, my mother had improved. I went back to Hartford, and she said, "Huh! Tell Bob I saved his life because he had to come home because I was going to die. That deserves a present."

When Bob was well enough, he came to Hartford to see her, and she said, "You owe me a present."

He said, "How about a trip around the world?"

She said, "You know I'm not well enough for that."

"Well, how about a box of candy?"

"You sure came down a lot!"

So that was their joke. A year and a half later, in August of 1999, I said to Bob, "I don't know how much longer she's going to live. I think you ought to come down to say goodbye."

We drove to Hartford. As we sat in my mother's room, I said to her, "Mom, do you know who this is?"

Her head was down. She said, "It's your husband." She couldn't remember his name. But all of a sudden her head went up, and she said, "You still owe me a present!"

That was classic. She always kept track of who owed her, who had called her and who hadn't. I knew then that she couldn't have had Alzheimer's.

She died a few months later, in January of 2000, at the age of almost 95. Every one of her grandchildren came to her funeral.

Even now, when I'm facing my own death, I believe that I would not be who I am if it hadn't been for my mother. Although I still get teary when I look back at my childhood, the tangles of our relationship and the tangible evidence that she could never really love me, I know that she gave me the strength and the drive to become myself.

CHAPTER NINE

THE OTHER SHOE DROPS

Dum Spiro Spero:
As long as I breathe, I hope.

- Latin proverb

After I had uterine cancer in 1975, I lived in fear of a recurrence. Every year, when I went for a checkup, I cleared my next day's calendar at work in case of bad news. Eventually, as the years rolled by, I began to relax. I really was cured. Any further cancer would not be related. Twenty-six years later, in February of 2001, I went to Gary Tanguay, our primary physician, for my annual checkup. When it came to the breast exam, he seemed to take an inordinately long time.

Finally, he said, "Lois, I want you to have a mammogram."

I said, "Gary, I don't need a mammogram. I had one recently." I faithfully scheduled and kept that appointment every year.

He said, "You need a mammogram."

Again, I said, "Gary, that's the silliest thing I've ever heard."

"Lois, would you please be the patient and let me be the doctor?"

I gave in and called Norman Sadowsky at Faulkner Hospital, who was not only a dear friend but also a renowned breast radiologist. Faulkner took me right away. I remember that day exactly. They did another mammogram, but nothing showed up; I had also had a negative mammogram five months before. (I later learned that 15% of all breast cancers don't show up on mammograms.) However, the technician could feel the same thing that Dr. Tanguay had. Norman said, "Lois, I think I'm going to do an ultrasound." So he did an ultrasound and he said, "You know, there's something there. It's a little cloudy, and I don't think it's anything. But I can't you let you go home without being sure, so I'm going to do a fine needle biopsy." So he did the fine needle biopsy. When I left, he said, "Don't worry. If there's anything there, it's not serious. I'll let you know tomorrow after it's read."

The next afternoon at one o'clock, I was getting ready to leave the house to do a board training for a charter school of Hispanics and Vietnamese in Lowell. There had been many problems between these two groups, and the city was trying to improve the relationship by bringing the children together to learn to work and play. As I was walking out the door, Norman called. I picked up the telephone and heard him say, "Lois, I can't believe it. You have invasive ductal carcinoma. You need to come in tomorrow." And so what did I do? I went on to Lowell as I had planned, did the training and came home. Only at that point did I call Bob, who was in Florida, and he came home.

Patty went with me to see Margaret Duggan, the wonderful surgeon whom Norman had recommended at Faulkner, and I carried with me twenty-one pages about breast cancer that I had printed from my Internet research. Dr. Duggan described my choices, and I said, "No, I have already decided. I want a lumpectomy." She told me that she usually asked people to go home and think about their options for a week before she let them make a decision, but in my case she knew it was all right to go ahead. The day she performed the lumpectomy, she came in after the surgery to tell us that she was 98% certain that the cancer had not spread to the lymph nodes. She would know for certain in five days, after the final pathology report was completed. Bob, the eternal optimist, heard the good news, took me home and went back to Florida two days later. I couldn't understand why he wouldn't wait for the report, but I didn't know yet that he was sick himself. His still undiagnosed lung cancer had resulted in a shortage of oxygen to his brain and affected his judgment.

He left for Florida on Sunday, and the following Tuesday I went to an appointment at UMass with Worcester oncologist Kathryn Edmiston. We were to discuss my treatment, focusing on the protocol typically followed when the lymph nodes were unaffected. Before she began, however, Kathy said, "Lois, I have to make sure that I know the results of the tests." She went out, she came back in, she looked at me and she said, "I have bad news. You are in the two percent; it's in your lymph nodes. You have to go back for more surgery to see how many nodes are involved."

Because I had to heal from the lumpectomy, they didn't schedule my next surgery for three weeks, and I went to Florida to join Bob. In April, Dr. Duggan did find lymph node involvement, which meant that I would have to have both chemotherapy and radiation. Again I called Bob, and this time I said, "Pack up now and come home." While I was waiting to heal so that I could start chemotherapy, Bob told me that he was having trouble swallowing. Sometimes when you get older and have trouble swallowing, all they have to do is put in a tube and expand the esophagus. So he was sent for an endoscopy. When I went to pick him up, the gastroenterologist said to me, "There's something there." Gary Tanguay called me, not Bob, to tell me that he was sending him to a pulmonologist. "There's something there," he told me, "and you'll handle it."

On the Thursday before Memorial Day weekend, we went to see the pulmonologist at Memorial. He looked at all the tests and told Bob, "I'm putting you in the hospital immediately, and tomorrow a surgeon will do a biopsy." Bob had just ordered a car, a Lexus. It wasn't new, it was at the end of a three-year lease; now that he was in Florida most of the time, he drove only to the office and the golf course. He had just transferred money so that he could pick up the car the day after Memorial Day. After the meeting with the doctor, as we rode up in the elevator to get him settled in the hospital room, I said, "You know, Bob, we'd better call Bancroft Motors and tell them to hold the car until we know what the biopsy says." Bob said, "Don't worry, if something's really bad, you'll be a widow with a Lexus." And I said, "Not me; I'm not driving around in a used Lexus. I'm going to get a brand new car." And we laughed. That was our typical sick humor for the next few months.

The next morning, very nauseated from my own chemo, I went to the hospital early in the morning. Bob had already gone to surgery for the biopsy. Soon, my daughters, Patty and Rachel, arrived. As we sat together in the waiting room, the surgeon came in and said, "I don't have good news. He has lung cancer."

"What does it mean?" I asked.

"Well," he said, "we'll have to wait to get the rest of the results from the lab, because this is just the initial diagnosis."

"Are you expecting something miraculous?"

"No."

So I said, "What are you talking about?"

And he said, "Six months to a year."

I asked him a few more questions, and he left. And then – only after he left – did I cry.

Bob came upstairs to his room, but he never asked about the results. I think he knew. I had this terrible burden of knowing that he was going to die, but I never said a word. An oncologist, Dr. Richard Horner, came in at one point over the weekend and asked if we wanted to go to Boston for further consultation, but Bob said no. Dr. Horner was wonderful and by our side for the next four months. That same weekend, Joe Moakley, the congressman from Boston, died. Everybody had loved Joe. We watched the funeral on television and cried because it brought back all of the memories of World War II, Bob's war. It was Memorial Day weekend, so it was particularly evocative. The nurses, the aides, the residents and interns all asked Bob, "Were you in the war?" When he said yes, and that he had been wounded, they said, "Thank you. Thank you for your service to the country." It was the most remarkable weekend, and it was very emotional for Bob.

By the time we got home, he knew how sick he was, though he was certain he was going to make it. The plan was to give him radiation to shrink the tumor in the center of his chest, followed up with chemotherapy. At home, he wasn't eating. I told him he had to eat, and he had to sit down to rest. He yelled at me for being such a terrible boss. So I said to myself, I understand, he's trying to deal with this terrible diagnosis. I told him that I had an errand to do. Then I got in my car and drove to Neal Rosenblum Goldsmiths, on Park Avenue, where I bought an incredibly expensive platinum bracelet.

When I walked in the house, Bob said in an angry voice, "Where were you?"

"I went to Neal's, and this is what I bought," I told him, showing him the bracelet. "It cost a fortune. Any time you yell at me I'm going to go out and buy myself a piece of jewelry, and, by the way, there are earrings to match."

Bob burst out laughing. That was the last time we ever had words.

It was a difficult summer, but we treasured the time together, and Bob was in wonderful spirits. All the pieces came together to allow us to conclude unfinished business, enjoy our children and grandchildren, and say goodbye to friends and family. I was quite sick for eleven of the twenty-one days between each of my six chemo treatments, but I took care of Bob, especially in the first weeks. At the beginning, we had an aide for just a few hours, someone whom Carol Seager, the most fabulous care manager and my very dear friend, found for us. But Bob eventually lost so much weight that he had to have a feeding tube put in, and I had to have more hours of help. Someone came in the morning and again at night. As sick as I was, I did things I never thought I could do. I changed him at night when he had accidents, learned to give him injections, fed him through the tube; I did everything. Once he had a blood clot, and I had to call the EMTs. He hated being in the hospital the few times he had to go. One night, I asked Bob, "Are you scared?" And he said, "No, 58 years ago I was lying wounded in the battlefield. I thought it was the end, so I had 58 wonderful years in between, and I have no fear." He really was extraordinary.

On July 23rd, on Bob's 76th birthday, we gathered the family together for a farewell birthday celebration. Bob said it was the best birthday he had ever had. The whole family came, and we held it in the backyard and on the porch, picnic-style. He was on oxygen at that point, but he put it aside and played Simon Says one last time with all of the children. A wonderful photographer from Worcester, Patrick O'Connor, came to take pictures. He only shot photos for annual reports, rather than birthday parties or weddings, but he came as a special favor to me. He stayed for three hours, taking pictures of all different groups of the family, and all he charged me for was the film. Hanging on the wall of my bedroom is a picture he took of all nineteen of us together, Bob at the very center. I treasure those pictures as a memory of that day.

In early September, however, Dr. Horner told us that the radiation they had given him to shrink the tumor had not been successful. They could not give him chemotherapy. Bob said, "Then this is the end? There's nothing more you can do for me?" I recall vividly that Dr. Horner pulled up a chair and held Bob's hands while he cried. It was an extraordinarily kind and warm gesture. It was at that point – when there was no more hope -- that Bob went on the downslide. There was nothing left for him to look forward to except dying.

On September 11, he didn't want to watch any of the televised coverage of the terrorist attacks on the World Trade Center. I said to him, "I need to watch it, but I also want to be with you." He said, "Then turn the TV away, and make it soft." The Visiting Nurse Association had given me materials, called "Gone From My Sight," that explained what to expect during the last weeks of life, and I knew then that Bob was beginning to leave me. It was not until the very last week that I had to put him in a hospital bed; his legs were very swollen. I said to him, "I am too weak to pick you up if you fall." He started to cry because he knew that was the end. At that point, I had aides around the clock.

Yom Kippur was on Thursday of that final week, and Bob was still coming downstairs, using the chairlift I had had installed. Patty, Alex and Laura were there from Wayland. I had told my brother, Joel, not to come, but he wouldn't be denied. He showed up with a sandwich and a soda so that I wouldn't have to feed him. Joel loved Bob, and he was determined to be there to say goodbye to him.

On Friday, the following night, I was scheduled to give a speech at Peter Levine's retirement party. I had read it to Bob a few days before, and he had told me it sounded good. During the day that Friday, he began to sleep a lot. Barbara and Nate Greenberg came to say goodbye to him, but he barely noticed.

That night, we started him on morphine, his first dose, because the nurse had said to him, "You're so uncomfortable because you're so bloated. The more we feed you, the less you're able to absorb it."

He said to her, "What does that mean?"

"You'll die sooner."

So he said, "Then stop feeding me."

I got dressed to go out, putting on a formal gown, and Bob made a circle with his thumb and forefinger to give me the signal that I looked wonderful. "If he dies," I said to the aide, "don't call me. But if there's an emergency, call me."

I went to the dinner and gave the speech, and by the time I came home he was out of it. I burst into tears, knowing that I couldn't share with Bob how good the speech had been or that they had given me a standing ovation. And I went to bed. At four o'clock in the morning, he woke up, and he said, "So how did it go?" I couldn't believe it. I pulled my chair over to his bed, and he wanted to know who was at the table and what they wore and what we ate and how the other speeches went and this and that. He was so proud of me, and he was chatting with the aide. He was comfortable and happy, and he wanted to get up and sit in the chair.

At 10 o'clock on Saturday morning, Gary Tanguay, our primary care physician, came to the house. Gary knew he had started Bob on morphine, and so he came upstairs to say goodbye. What doctor does that? Bob had had only the one shot of morphine, I believe, and he didn't think he was in any pain, but he couldn't lie on his back. He said the sheets hurt him. Bob was sitting in the chair, Gary was on our bed, and they were joking and laughing. They were both golf nuts. Bob said, "You know, I'd like a root beer." He loved root beer. And Gary said, "You can have one." So I went downstairs, and I got him a root beer. He drank it, and he said, "Well, I would really like a Reuben," and Gary said, "With sauerkraut?" Bob said, "No, it gives me gas." So Gary said, "You can have one." And he said, "No, I guess I couldn't swallow it." Then they told a hilarious story about the time Bob brought me perfume from a golf trip to Florida.

"Where the hell were you?" I had asked when I had discovered the box read "duty free."

"In Miami Beach," he had said innocently.

I only had to ask a few pointed questions about where he had stayed and where he had eaten to deduce that he and his friend had actually gone to Cuba for the weekend. When they woke up to the sound of gunshots and Castro's voice on a loudspeaker, they had decided it was time to go home.

Bob loved to tell the story about my detective work.

When Gary left that Saturday morning, I walked him out, and he said, "You take care of *yourself*. You haven't had any time to do that."

I went back upstairs, and Bob's head was down. I didn't know it yet, but he had fallen into a coma. That afternoon, Rachel came with little Daniel, who was only seven months old. The book I had read about the final hours said that Bob could still hear, so Rachel talked to him. I called my friends, Randy and Michael Wertheimer, who were both doctors. They were at a party in Worcester that night, and they came over and confirmed that he was in a coma. This was at six-thirty in the evening. When he left, Michael Wertheimer said, "Goodbye, Bob." So I knew.

I was absolutely exhausted. Rachel went to her room with Daniel, and I said to the aide, "I'm going to sleep in the other room and catch a couple of winks. All the lights are on in here, and I'm so tired. Call me immediately if anything changes." I don't think I had been asleep for five minutes when she came in to tell me that Bob had died. It was eleven o'clock.

I had the Comfort Care/DNR verification posted on the refrigerator, so we didn't have to call the EMTs. Instead, we called the VNA, who came and declared him dead, and then Perlman's, the funeral home. Rachel and I sat up and talked until they took him away, and then we went back to bed to try to get some sleep for a few hours.

We couldn't have the funeral on Sunday, because Sarah was in California and couldn't get here quickly enough. Tuesday was Sukkot, so that meant that Bob couldn't be buried until Wednesday. By that time, everybody would be able to arrive. I was finished with my own chemo treatments by then and had been scheduled to begin radiation. On Tuesday, I had an appointment to be marked up for the treatments. That morning, I got in the car and went to the hospital. I had no intention of missing a single moment of my radiation because I wanted to go to Florida with my kids for Thanksgiving. Nobody could believe that I went, but I was on a schedule. Everybody in the radiation department cried. They had all loved Bob.

The funeral was incredible. Bob had been a president of Temple Emanuel, and was known throughout the community. The sanctuary was packed. Stanley Davids, a former rabbi at Temple Emanuel, had come up from Atlanta to be part of the service because I was very close to him, and Jordan Millstein, our rabbi, officiated. My son, David, gave the eulogy. When Rabbi Davids followed, he said, "After David, I feel superfluous." Rabbi Millstein said a few words, and then we went to the cemetery.

At the suggestion of his nurse, I had gone to Perlman's with Barbara Greenberg the day before Bob died to choose his coffin and to arrange the funeral. (While I was there, I had told them to do the very same for me when my time came.) I gave Richie Perlman the obituary I had written at three o'clock in the morning one night in August when I couldn't sleep. When I mentioned that Bob had been wounded in World War II and had received a Purple Heart, Richie asked me, "Do you know that there is a regiment in upstate New York that travels to the funerals of World War II veterans with Purple Hearts and performs a ceremony? Would you like that?" I thought for a minute. I wasn't sure whether it was tacky or not. But I said yes. I didn't say anything to the children.

As we stood in the cemetery on Wednesday, five soldiers appeared in the far distance. They marched towards us down the gravel path and, when they reached us, stood in formation while the bugler blew "Taps." They then came over to the gravesite, held the flag at each of its four corners and folded it into a triangle. When the soldier presented it to me, he said "Thank you for his service to the country." That moment was so important for my grandchildren, so that they could understand what kind of man their Pop-pop had been. That night, when everybody came back to the house for the service, Jordan Millstein asked people to tell stories about Bob instead of just doing a service in the home. It was really wonderful.

The day after the funeral, I started radiation. And then, only a month later, my daughter, Sarah, in California called to tell me that she had been diagnosed with bi-lateral breast cancer. I couldn't go out to take care of her because I was sick, and she wasn't going to be able to come to Florida in November. I felt terrible. At that point, I went to be tested for the BR CA1 and

BR CA2 genes for breast cancer. I had two other daughters, and even sons with the gene are predisposed to early prostate cancer. Both Sarah and I tested negative, but everyone remains convinced that there has to be some sort of genetic connection. (At this point, Sarah continues to do well.)

That was 2001. And I was glad to see the end of it.

The next year, I sold our house on Rutland Terrace, where we had lived for 48 years, and moved to a retirement community in Holden called the Seasons. Bob and I had been thinking about moving for a while, but every time he looked out the window and saw the grandchildren playing in our backyard, he changed his mind. Finally, in 2000, we made the decision to leave. We didn't want to move too far away, and we both liked the plans for the Seasons. I also knew the reputation of the builder. We tried to put down a deposit, but at that point the planning board hadn't yet approved the project. The following year, we were both sick, but we put down a deposit anyway. There wasn't a model to look at yet, and so I picked the site by the location and the big driveway. All that summer, I chose tiles, flooring etc. Every time I asked Bob what he thought, he said it was up to me. He knew he wasn't going to get there, but I picked the largest unit anyway to make room for the hospital bed. I ended up moving in June of 2002, even before my house had sold; there were very few residents at the time.

My plan was to spend part of my year in Holden and the winter months in Florida. Bob had always wanted to make that our routine, and now I decided that it was time. Wherever I was, I found myself busier than ever. In Longboat Key, I quickly made new friends in addition to those I had known. Twenty years earlier, in a wonderful coincidence, I had run across a picture of a woman named Barbara Saphier in the Sarasota newspaper; she looked very much like my friend, Bobbie Bernstein, from prep school. I called her up and left a message: "If this is the Bobbie Bernstein who went to Drew Seminary, please call me. Otherwise, I'm sorry to have bothered you." Twenty minutes later, the phone rang and heard a woman say, "Lois! I don't believe it!" It was the same person. We reconnected, and once I decided to stay in Sarasota for six months each year, we could spend more time together. It was Bobbie who introduced me to many of my new friends. I joined a book group, took classes, and slowly began to participate in a number of activities. I don't play tennis or golf, swim in the pool or sit in the sun. But it's warm, and I love the Gulf. To me, being able to wake up in the morning and look at the water is therapeutic. It's nourishing; it feeds my soul.

In Worcester, I continued my work as a consultant to boards, agencies and individuals. My involvement with the Geriatric Clerkship at UMass Medical School began in 2002 and has become an important, if short-term, part of my life. In conjunction with my roles as trustee for the Hoche Scofield Foundation and Clark University, I have not only maintained but also deepened my connection and commitment to the community.

That has been particularly true of my association with the United Way. In 2000, the year before Bob and I both got sick, I received a phone call from two men who wanted to take me to lunch at the Worcester Club. It was a Friday, and they wanted to see me immediately. It was urgent, they said, and involved the United Way.

I wasn't free that day, but they kept pressing me, and I

suggested meeting them on Monday after work for a drink. All weekend, I kept thinking about the upcoming conversation. I was certain that they wanted me to step in as Executive Director. The organization was in flux at the time. As I mulled it over, I began to think that I would like such a position. I role-played and prepared, trying to figure out the salary I should request.

Finally, we met, and they said, "Lois, we've been so impressed with your commitment to the United Way. We'd like you to be the first woman to run the campaign."

I said, "Oh, my God. Here I've been spending the weekend trying to decide how much money I would ask of you, and you're asking me to do something that will probably cost me money!"

They laughed.

When I got home, I called Bob in Florida, where he was spending a few days.

"What do you think?" I asked him. "I'd be the first woman to do it. We don't give a lot of money, but they want me to do it anyway. I think I could do a good job. But I told them I wouldn't give them an answer until I had talked to you."

He started to laugh. "Now why should this night be different from any other night? Of course you're going to take it. You've already made that decision. And I'll be there for you."

I was so touched to have been asked. Usually, the campaign chairman is a big wheel in the community, the head of a big corporation or a bank or somebody who gives a lot of money. My own financial commitment to the United Way had been relatively minimal. I ran the campaign with as much ardor as I could, and I loved it. I was tireless, fearlessly asking for money. I was determined to set new ground. In the end, we raised seven million dollars, and I don't think they've ever gone that high again. Once again, I had an opportunity to meet and get involved with all of the wonderful people in the community who had devoted their lives to Greater Worcester. Everybody received me graciously, and I was treated with respect everywhere I went. After the campaign, Bob gave me a beautiful star necklace because he said I was a star.

In December 2001, I was in Longboat Key and read an article in the newspaper about the United Way of Sarasota. The list of new volunteers included a chairman of something named the "Women's Initiative." I called the organization and asked to speak to someone about it. The Executive Director and the staff person involved took me to lunch. They explained that the concept called for women to work together to raise their own funds for a specific focus. They had picked scholarships for day care.

I returned to Worcester, certain this approach would be ideal for our own community. On a small scale, I had personally witnessed the impact of that kind of direct service. In the late 1990s, when I first became a trustee at Clark, I wanted to make a gift, but nothing they suggested appealed to me. Eventually, someone asked whether I would like to do something that improved the Main South neighborhood where Clark is located. My eyes lit up. That was the beginning of the Robert F and Lois B. Green Internship Fund. Every summer, the fund gives a stipend to a Clark student who spends the summer working in Main South. Some have worked in the city councilor's office, others for different agencies. They do research and write a paper. Every September, I meet with the student and hear about what he or she has accomplished.

From that Clark experience, I knew that a Women's Initiative, focused on targeting and addressing specific issues, would have broad appeal and a positive influence in Worcester. Women give differently from men; they want to see where their money is going, they want to be directly involved, and they want to make sure it's going to the right cause. According to a brief on women and philanthropy from several years ago, women want to create, change, connect, commit, collaborate and celebrate. To get started, in 2003, I met with a few women leaders -- some active in the United Way, others not -- to ask their opinion. The general consensus was that women in Central Massachusetts wanted control of their philanthropy, they wanted to make a measurable difference on issues that were important to them, and they wanted to be educated about issues affecting their community. They were especially interested in addressing the needs of women and children.

Some of the women with whom I spoke argued for starting a separate women's fund, but I wanted to create such an initiative in collaboration with rather than in competition with the United Way. When I broached the subject with the Executive Director, he was completely supportive. There was considerable concern on the part of the staff that the Women's Initiative would take away money that would have gone to the larger campaign. However, I insisted that we would actually bring in more money; we were going to ask people to give to the Women's Initiative in addition to whatever they intended to give to the United Way.

And so we started. Adopting the mantra of women's philanthropy, that women give their "time, talent and treasure," Meridith Wesby, whom I asked to co-chair with me, and I met with focus groups and put together a steering committee of 22. We hired a "star," Kate Myshrall, to staff the program, and we could not have found a more committed or dedicated leader. I have never known anyone who works harder than Kate. From the start, the steering committee set the minimum donation for membership at $100 rather than the more typical $1000 or $10,000 of other United Way women's groups. Other Women's Initiatives were (and continue to be) based on big giving, but the women in Worcester wanted to be fully inclusive, embracing women from all walks of life, not merely those with the greatest resources. Indeed, a more grassroots style of organization can be just as effective, giving a broader range of the population a greater stake in the outcome for the community.

The committee narrowed the focus of the initiative first to women and girls, and then further to the issues facing adolescent girls. Not only was there little programming in the area for girls from ages 10 to 14, but agencies and schools also found that girls of that age tended to disappear from programming that did exist. The Women's Initiative planned to make a difference for young girls by funding programs that could provide both skills and positive influences at a critical time in their development.

180 women attended our first event, and we raised $43,000. Middle school girls themselves had already told us that they were most concerned about teen pregnancy, alcohol and substance abuse, suicide and depression, and violence. At our event, we circulated a ballot among the attendees, asking them to choose one of those areas as the focus for the Initiative's first year. They selected violence. At the same time, we recruited members to join one (or several) of our working committees: Coordinating, Planning, Fundraising and Distribution.

As the organization has grown, we have come to recognize just how powerful a weapon greater self-esteem can be against violence in the home, in the schools, and in the community. To that end, Hanover Insurance Company gave us a large grant to organize a training around financial literacy for girls in the community. We followed a curriculum about how to use and understand money, teaching women to mentor the girls at a two-day intensive workshop. The purpose has been to educate girls about financial self-sufficiency so that they can protect themselves from the repercussions of violence.

We do some training around issues involving boys, who are often responsible for the violence, but we are also concerned about girls bullying girls. We have been very fortunate to receive grants from local philanthropist, Val Loring. (Val and I have been friends and neighbors for many years. She was a United Way team captain with me at the very beginning.) Her generosity has allowed us to bring in excellent speakers, among them Mary Pipher, author of *Raising Ophelia*, and Rosalind Wiseman, the author of *Queen Bees and Wannabees: Helping Your Daughter Survive Cliques, Gossip, Boyfriends, and Other Realities of Adolescence*.

The Women's Initiative has grown exponentially, allowing us to say to any woman, "Join us, serve on the allocations committee, the campaign committee, the planning committee, volunteer as a mentor for a day." We don't turn anyone down. At our sixth year anniversary, at an event held in October 2008, 1200 participants raised over $360,000. Even though membership remains set at $100, we now have 90 members who give $1000 or more. Since its inception, the Women's Initiative has promoted greater awareness of the issue of violence not only through programs and presentations but also through the direct involvement of girls themselves, giving them a personal connection with active and intelligent women in our community. Several years ago, our organization won a national award, and a few of us traveled to accept it. It was very exciting.

To me, the most exhilarating aspect of the Women's Initiative has not been the specific issue addressed, but rather the extraordinary power of women to come together. To see women reach a consensus about a need in the community that we felt we could improve, raise the necessary funds, evaluate proposed projects, allocate and oversee the money, and celebrate our success has been far more important than the specific focus area. There are a lot of needs in the community. We could have focused on the homeless, on teenage boys, on hunger. The real significance of the Women's Initiative is its demonstration that women can institute change and have an enormous impact on an area -- any area -- of community concern. I think what makes me the happiest is the involvement of the young women who are coming after me. It will be in good hands, and it will continue.

In May of 2005, while I was still deeply involved with the Women's Initiative, I met once more with representatives from the United Way. The President and CEO was about to resign, and I was asked if I would serve as interim. I was dumbfounded. I was 75 years old. Then I thought, why not? You've never been a president or CEO of anything. Wouldn't that be neat? As we discussed the salary, I told them, "I will only take the position if you give me the same rights and privileges as you would a full-time president and CEO. I want the ability to hire, fire and make changes, and I do not want to be second-guessed by the

Board." They agreed.

Because I had already been chairman of the board and campaign chairman, as well as the chairman of allocations, they didn't need to train me. I went to work soon after on a Tuesday in early June. That morning, as I got ready to leave, I felt a lump on the other breast, the one that had not had the lumpectomy four years before. I had been checked a month earlier by the oncologist, who said I was fine. I also had had my annual physical and had been told that everything was fine. So I realized that this large lump had to have grown in just two weeks or a month. When I arrived at the office, I called my oncologist, and she gave me an appointment for Thursday morning.

That day, I told my staff I wasn't sure how long I would be gone. Dr. Edmiston felt the lump and said, "Oh, darn." I knew it had to be bad because it had grown so fast. She sent me for a biopsy right away, down on the first floor. The person who did the biopsy asked if I wanted to know the results right away or if I wanted to go home and have them call me. I said I wanted to know immediately. "Is it okay if we tell you instead of the doctor?" "Yes," I said, "You have my permission." So they did the biopsy, and the results were to take only fifteen minutes. I waited, and I waited, and I waited. I never let them shut the door on me in any examining room because I hate being closed in; I like seeing people go by. So, after maybe thirty minutes, I saw the technician walking down the hall with Kathy Edmiston. They had had to wait until she could leave to come downstairs. I knew immediately. She looked at me -- this was now the second time she had given me bad news -- and I said, "You don't have to say anything."

She said, "I'm sending you over for a mammogram and an ultrasound and I've got an appointment for you at five-thirty with Dr. Quinlan." He was the surgeon who had taken care of Bob at an earlier surgery, and I also knew him from when I was on the hospital board. I have enormous respect for him, and he is incredibly kind. After I had the additional tests, I went back to my office at the United Way and told them that I had had some bad news. I didn't know how long I would be able to serve as interim. I called the chairman of the board to fill him in, telling him that I intended to try my best but that I wasn't sure how the next few months would progress.

Patty met me at Dr. Quinlan's office. It was late, after hours, and most of the offices were dark. Dr. Quinlan came out of his office, and he said, "I can't believe this is happening to you. You don't deserve this, especially after all the work you've done for the hospital." Then he hugged me. He drew me a picture of where the cancer was and told me that I needed surgery right away. He had had a cancellation for the following Tuesday and had saved me the spot if I wanted it. I said, "Schedule me. I'm not going to look for a second opinion." I knew how fast this cancer had grown. It was a new primary site, so he did another lumpectomy; this time, the cancer had not spread to my lymph nodes. "Good," I said. "All I'm going to need is radiation." Kathy Edmiston said, "Yes, all you need is radiation. But the tests aren't back yet."

I went back to see her for a follow up appointment, and for the third time she told me bad news. I didn't have any of the positive receptors. There are three receptors for breast cancer: estrogen, progesterone, and HER 2. When you have those, you can have all the new forms of chemo; you can take Tamoxifen.

(You can also do radiation without chemotherapy, at least if you've had a lumpectomy.) I was triple negative, about as bad a situation as there was in terms of treatment. During that fall and winter, I had chemo first and then radiation, and I never missed a day of work. I lost my hair again and had a wig, and it was just as traumatic as it had been the first time.

Everyone told me how wonderful I was to continue to work under those circumstances, but I said, "I came in to the United Way when they needed me desperately, and the United Way came into my life when I needed them desperately." To have a reason to get up and go to work in the morning when I was struggling, going through chemotherapy, was extraordinary.

My primary task was to rebuild the campaign, but I soon realized that the staff also needed support. I cared about them, and I wanted them to have a good experience. The first day I was there, I met with them all, a group of about 30. I told them what my hopes were for our time together and that I wanted to know their hopes as well. I sent each staff member a one-page sheet and asked them to describe their position as it was, then what they wanted to do, the obstacles in the way of achieving their goals, and the help they needed to get there. I got back these wonderful responses, and then I sat down to meet with each of them individually. It worked very well. The feeling was very similar to Elder Home Care. I cared about all of them, I knew where they were and who had babysitting troubles etc. In return, they were magnificent to me. When I had my 75th birthday that August, they had a great party for me, with a proclamation from the mayor and all sorts of wonderful gifts.

I also got along well with the board. I suspect that one reason I was as successful as I was during those months was that

I knew everybody from having been campaign chairman five years earlier. I went out and met with the CEO of every major company and every bank, many of whom I already knew. To be honest, I have to admit that I occasionally used my being sick. I was planning to meet with the vice presidents of St. Gobain, and they suggested a certain date. I said, "Oh, I'm sorry, I can't do it on that day. I'm having chemotherapy." I figured a little sympathy would go a long way.

When I did go to St. Gobain, our biggest contributor, I discovered that they were upset with the United Way and intended to cut their usual gift. I told them the same thing I said to others: "We are looking for a new president and CEO. There is only so much I can achieve now, but don't give up on me and let me see what I can do." To a person, they all agreed. When St. Gobain said, "Okay, we won't cut your gift," I remember looking up and saying, "Oh! I thought you were going to increase it!" They all laughed. Only I could get away with something like that.

I had someone else call a breakfast meeting with the heads of all the local foundations. I belonged to that foundation group myself, but I didn't feel that it was appropriate for me to put the meeting together under these circumstances. They had all been very supportive of the United Way for years, but they gave me a very hard time about what was wrong with the organization. At the time, the United Way had moved away from raising funds to a newer concept of community impact. The community didn't understand what that approach meant and was concerned that the organization had lost its way. Again, I told them I had discovered quite a few problems and that I hoped to accomplish certain things. And I asked them not to give up on us. About ten days later, I received a contribution from one of the foundations that had never before given to the United Way; it was not part of their own mission. They told me that they planned from then on to give annually to the campaign and included a separate check to help us with the search for new leadership.

One day, I was having chemo when a woman came in and said, "I heard you were having chemo today, and I wondered if I could sit next to you." I knew her very well. In fact, we had both been door-to-door solicitors for the United Way years before. So, she sat next to me, and I opened the curtain. She wanted to tell me how impressed she was that I had done so much for the United Way, given how sick I was. She then proceeded to rattle off everything she thought was wrong with the organization.

In my best social worker demeanor – not being a social worker – I said, "Thank you so much for sharing that. Those are the same issues that are near and dear to my heart, and I am trying to address many of them. I can't do them all in the short time before we hire a full-time CEO."

And then I continued. "By the way," I said. "I know you've given gifts to the United Way and belong to the Women's Initiative, but I'd like you to make a gift of $1000."

She asked, "Lois, are you soliciting me while I'm having chemotherapy?"

I said, "Yes! You can't hang up the telephone on me, and you can't walk out on me because you're hooked up to a machine."

She smiled and laughed and said, "Okay, I'll give it to you."

She gave me permission to share that story, which I love

to tell.

I was supposed to serve as interim for only four months, but by November, the search had still not turned up a new president and CEO. I wanted to go to Florida for the winter, and so I made a deal with the board. I would spend the first two weeks of every month in Worcester, which allowed me to attend executive committee, finance committee and board meetings. I would then work from Florida during the second two weeks of the month. They didn't want to hire a new interim CEO, and so they agreed. I supervised my staff one-on-one on the telephone. They called me every day with problems, and of course I had my computer. I could call or email people, and no one would actually know where I was. I did that until April, when the new President and CEO was in place and could step forward. At that point, I decided to back off from the organization and allow the new executive some space, though I did continue to be involved with the Women's Initiative.

The following year, the United Way called again and asked me to do some training for the campaign workers. With Linda Cavioli, I ran three or four very successful workshops that focused on how to solicit for funds. I ran a similar workshop for the Women's Initiative. I keep trying to step back, but my heart is there. I want them to do well, so I continue to respond when they ask me for help. I suppose until I die that organization will have a soft spot in my heart because so much of my life and my time have been spent with the United Way.

In many ways, the United Way has helped me to refine my own interpretation of community service. Several years ago, I was honored by the Planned Giving Council, which named me "Philanthropist of the Year." At the time, I thought it was pretty funny. As far as I knew, a philanthropist gave millions of dollars and had buildings named after him or her. To be considered a philanthropist for the small amounts I had been able to contribute was certainly an error in judgment. However, the more I thought about it, the more I began to realize that I was indeed a philanthropist. I volunteer my time, I share my talent doing the things that I do well, and I give my treasure to the best of my ability. Indeed, the Women's Initiative exemplifies philanthropy, as each of our members gives of her own time, talent and treasure. Without a doubt, our success has demonstrated the power of women to make a difference, with the vision and tenacity necessary to evaluate and address the issues critical for community growth.

CHAPTER TEN

CHOOSE LIFE

"I call heaven and earth to witness against you today that I have set before you life and death, blessings and curses. Choose life so that you and your descendants may live."

- Deuteronomy 30:19

In 2006, when I was still working at the United Way, Reyna Lounsbury, my former student from the Geriatric Clerkship, and another nursing student came down to Florida so they could videotape an interview with me for a class on chronic illness. On the tape, I said I knew that my cancer was coming back. The following winter, in 2007, I made an appointment with Caryn Silver, an oncologist in Florida. When she asked me why I was there, I told her that I needed a local doctor. I was certain the cancer would return, and I didn't want to have to run up to Massachusetts if I felt a lump.

That spring, I returned home and, in July, went to see Kathy Edmiston for a checkup. I told her that I had vertigo, probably from an inner ear infection that was making me nauseous and dizzy. She sent me for a brain scan, because breast cancer can metastasize to the brain, lungs, liver or bones. When she called me to tell me that the scan had been normal, she asked me how I was.

I said, "You know, Kathy, when I walk up the stairs, I've got to stop to catch my breath. I'm out of shape; I just need to get back to my trainer and start walking again."

She said, "Lois, I have to have you checked. I will never forgive myself if something is going on, and I didn't follow up."

This time, she sent me for a CT scan.

For the fourth time, she had to give me bad news. She said, "The cancer has metastasized to your lungs. You've got a tumor on one lung and two small ones on the other lung. We won't know what treatment you're going to need until we find out which cancer it is." I had had two different primary breast cancers, and this metastasis could have stemmed from either the 2001 or 2005 occurrence.

I had a lung biopsy and went back to see Kathy. Once more, now for the fifth time, she said, "Bad news. It's the cancer that never got to your lymph nodes."

This was the cancer that had been triple negative, and so, once again, I couldn't have any of the new hormonal therapies. I had no positive receptors. As a result, I had to do chemotherapy yet again.

I said, "Kathy, I'm 77 years old, and I am not going to be sick any more. And I don't want to lose my hair again."

"Okay," she said, "There is a chemo pill and a chemo that is infused."

"Which one can I drink wine with?"

"Both," she told me.

So I chose the pill, which gave me strange head tremors. I

didn't have any of the usual side effects, but the tremors were like having little seizures. I couldn't go into Target or anywhere with bright lights because they would set off a seizure. I stopped driving. Kathy reduced the dose, and I went off to Florida and stayed on this pill all winter. A CT scan in December in Florida showed no change, but another one when I returned to Massachusetts in the spring told us that the tumors had grown.

"We have to take you off the Xeloda," Kathy said.

In May of 2008, I began another treatment that she suggested. By August, the tumors had shrunk, though there appears to have been minimal growth since then. I am fatigued and occasionally have to have transfusions to address low blood counts, but I am back to walking for exercise. In September 2008, I walked the mile in the UMass Walk for Cancer. I'd be very happy if this could be my reality forever. Nonetheless, I know that the problem with chemotherapy – any chemo -- is that sooner or later it can stop working.

Last fall, I said to Kathy Edmiston, "Kathy, I've got to last until May because my granddaughter Becca is having her bat mitzvah. Besides, I have too much to do."

She laughed. "Lois, you can't tell me that," she said. "You always have too much to do. That will always be your excuse. And then you'll have to live forever."

In the meantime, I don't mind going for my treatment. I know everybody there, and they are all so kind to me. After many of my treatments, they ask me where I am going next. Once, when I was going right on to Boston to speak, I brought my speech to go over while I was having chemo; the staff made copies of it for themselves. They all have my talks, they all want to know how it went; it's like a little home away from home for me. After all, this is my third round. Everyone is so loving and caring that you feel as though you are the only person they are treating.

After my first round in 2001, I couldn't bear it that there were no clocks in the infusion rooms. When I asked about it, they said nobody had ever considered putting up clocks. So I took the clock off my oncologist's wall, called my dear friend, Jenique Leblond from the Development Office, and asked her to come right over. (Her office was right nearby.) "I want you to buy 29 clocks for me," I told Jenique. "I don't want a plaque, I just want clocks." So she bought clocks. When I went back the second time around, there were my clocks in every room. One of the staff members told me that everybody loved the clocks. They hadn't been sure that people would like them. Well, of course! Everyone wants to know what time it is. When you're attached to the infusion machine, you can't always look at your watch.

So now when I walk in, everybody says, "Here comes Lois. Do we have any problems we want to tell her about?" Not long ago, one of the nurses told me about two pamphlets she gives to new cancer patients, one about chemotherapy and the other about nutrition. She only gets ten a month for free. She had had 30 patients that particular month, and there was no money to buy extra pamphlets to meet the demand. They were only a nickel apiece!

I thought that was ridiculous. I gave her $20 and told her to buy 400 of them.

Then once again I called the Development Office. "I want to start a fund," I told them. "I'm not going to put in much money but I'm going to email everybody I know to send in $10 or $25. That will create a fund where they can buy booklets, for God's sake."

I went to a Pink event for breast cancer the following Thursday night and told the story to a couple of people who were big wheels at the hospital. They said, "Oh, we have money for that." I said, "Fine. I'm going to start the fund because I don't trust anybody. If you can get the money for pamphlets, great, and if you can't, they'll still have money to buy them."

One day, I met a woman while I was getting a CT scan. She wore a scarf, and she sat down next to me. I don't look as though I am going through chemo because I haven't lost my hair. I asked, "Are you struggling with breast cancer?" And we began to talk. At the time, Kathy was 47 years old. She had a sixteen-year-old daughter, who asked her, "Will you be here when I get married?" She had to say, "No, I can't be." There wasn't any more chemo that would work for her. We sat there and cried, the two of us. We exchanged phone calls and had lunch together. The staff knew that I was in touch with her, and I told them, "You know, I can call her, but what if she doesn't answer? What if something happens? I'm not going to know and you're not allowed to tell me." During the many phone calls Kathy and I exchanged, I had a chance to talk to her sister. I gave her all my numbers, and when Kathy died this past February, it was her sister who called me.

I keep trying to tell people that it's okay to talk frankly with me about dying. Instead, they say, "Oh, Lois, you're going to beat it. With your strength, you're going to be fine." Or, "We're all old. We can die anytime. After all, Lois, you could get killed by a bus while you're crossing the street."

What do you say in response? I have stopped trying. Knowing that I have stage 4 metastatic breast cancer, that I am having palliative treatment, that the three tumors are alive and well and that I will never be in remission makes my situation very different. It is not the same as acknowledging that we all are getting older and MAY die at any moment. I realize others cannot possibly understand. How could they? I hope they will never know what it feels like to go to sleep every night and wake up each morning saying to myself, "Good job, Lois. You made it one more day. Now get up and enjoy today!" A woman once told me, "Stay with us as long as you can." This may be the best thing anyone has said to me.

In the meantime, I am busier than I have ever been in my life – and that is saying something. In the past two and a half years, I have given quite a few speeches and presentations on end-of-life issues and how I would like my doctors to communicate with me; mentored those who have asked for my advice both formally and informally; and continued to participate in the organizations that matter most to me. In the late summer of 2008, I went to Toronto with my friend, Betty Brudnick, to attend a week-long Classical Pursuits workshop on Shakespeare. Whether in Massachusetts or in Florida, I have said yes to endless invitations for dinner, lunch, concerts, operas, movies and plays with my friends, both new and old. In Florida, I have a wonderful group of friends in Sarasota, another group in Longboat Key and another group with whom I go to exercise class. No matter where I am, I continue to make new friends, and I am always grateful for that wonderful moment of connection, so often unexpected. Since I was diagnosed this last time, we have had two glorious family celebrations at Thanksgiving in Florida, and look forward to another in a few months. In addition, I have loved having the chance to visit with my children and my grandchildren at every possible opportunity.

We all face difficult and painful challenges, but we each have a choice in determining how we respond to them. Some of us become so sad and depressed that we give up, turning inward and continually asking "why me?" Others deal with the reality of what is, look forward and move on. No one was more surprised than I to observe my own positive response to my personal health crises. I always considered myself the quintessential coward. Even the sight of blood made me queasy. Yet from my first cancer diagnosis in 1975 to my fourth and most recent bout, my journey of self-discovery has taught me that adversity only makes me stronger. With each new blow, I have become even more determined to look ahead and find something new and interesting to do. Instead of making me fearful, my difficulties have only made me more resolute, unwavering in my effort to make the most of every day: to savor the changing seasons, watch the sun set over the Gulf of Mexico, take pleasure in listening to a beautiful concert, relish my friendships and the love of my family.

In a strange way, I'm not sorry about my diagnosis. I'd like to live, but at the same time I have learned so much over the years from having cancer. I know now to enjoy things, to love everything I'm doing. It's not that I'm brave. I'm not really brave. I don't know what the ending's going to be like. I would like not to die. But I hope I have showed people how to live, and now perhaps it is time to show them how to die.

For the past few years, I have been able to do just that through my involvement in the Better Ending Partnership. When Bob was dying, I learned how very important it is to be able to make critical decisions about end of life while you are still able. Bob relied on me to communicate with everyone for him. I asked questions that he couldn't or wouldn't about his treatment, the outcome, the alternatives. Our physicians, VNA nurse, care manager and aides were with us through every step of his illness and death. I am forever grateful for the openness and support I received then and expect nothing less for myself. Like Bob, I too, want to be able to share with my doctors my concerns and fears and to know that they will be listening and responding to me. After he died, I took steps to ensure that my caregivers and my family know exactly what my wishes are.

In 2002, Dr. H. Brownell Wheeler, retired chief of surgery at UMass Medical Center, and community leader William Densmore formed the Central Massachusetts Partnership to Improve Care at the End of Life. The organization, which became a non-profit in 2004 and was renamed the Better Ending Partnership in 2007, was a coalition made up of representatives from relevant sectors of the community, including health care, social service, the legal profession, and faith groups. For its first three years, its intention was to educate the community on the importance of end-of-life decisions and health care proxies by working with lawyers, social workers, the clergy, employers and funeral directors, with special attention to cultural differences. For that initial period, the partnership was supported by seed money from the Worcester Foundations.

I joined the board of Better Ending in 2005 and served as chairman in 2007. In 2005, Dr. David Kaufman from St. Vincent's Hospital, along with other members of the Better Endings work group on health care, conducted the Sodium study (Snapshot of Dying in an Urban Milieu). They surveyed the immediate relatives of those who had died the year before, seeking to examine their experiences with existing end-of-life care in Worcester. The results made it clear that patients in Worcester were not dying in a place of their choice, nor was there adequate pain management. Family members did not feel that there had been adequate communication between their loved ones and their health care professionals. Few had been offered the option of hospice care. Finally, respondents indicated that health care proxies or DNR orders, where in place, had made for better care and recommended that such forms be encouraged.

Based on the Sodium study, Better Ending honed its focus to target specific areas, including hospice and palliative care services, symptom management, and end-of-life care in nursing homes. Supported by the Worcester health institutions as well as Blue Cross/Blue Shield, Better Endings has accomplished a range of tasks, including identifying barriers within the hospital and primary care settings that limit referrals for hospice and/or palliative care as well as the use of health care proxies. A Better Ending video was developed to use in nursing homes. Outreach efforts brought community professionals into the discussion. Through presentations throughout the community, the development of a website, educational programs and, especially the distribution of close to 120,000 copies of *A Guide for a Better Ending*, a pamphlet geared to "Conversations before the Crisis," Better Endings has reached thousands of people.

Late in the summer of 2008, after months spent trying to raise the funds to keep us going for the year and sustain us in years to come, we made the painful decision to dissolve Better Endings as a discrete entity. Instead, we turned to the health care institutions that had so generously supported us to take over the work we were doing and planning to do. I personally met with John O'Brien, CEO of UMass Memorial Health Care (UMMHC), Michael Collins, Chancellor of UMass Medical School, Tom Manning, Deputy Chancellor of Commonwealth Medicine, Eric Schultz, CEO of the Fallon Community Health Plan, and Jack Dutzar, CEO of the Fallon Clinic. They were all welcoming, supportive and encouraging. My own wish was to ensure that no single institution would own the project, but that it would remain a coalition, with the data to be shared with all. Representatives from each of these institutions have been meeting to discuss the transition and prepare for the transfer. The Better Ending website will be maintained by UMMHC, while at the same time retaining its community focus. The community engagement that was the original mission of Better Ending will continue under the aegis of Commonwealth Medicine. I have been thrilled to witness this willingness to work together, share information and outcomes, collaborate rather than compete. The biggest winner will be our community, the patients and families facing end-of-life decisions. Suzanna Makowski, Chief of Palliative Care at UMass Memorial, recently shared a meditation story with me. A clap, she said, is a sudden, sharp and loud noise that ends abruptly. In contrast, a bell rings softly, and its sound goes on and on. Like the sounding of a bell, the work of Better Ending Partnership will resonate for many years to come.

As for me, my personal wish, which I have shared with my oncologist and my children, is that I will die at home with my loved ones around me. As I told a newspaper reporter several months ago, "I already know I'm going out of here with my family by my side and a glass of wine in my hand." I believe that is the most humane ending one could hope for. As much as I like to be in control, even I know that I can't control my ending, so I have done whatever I could to facilitate it. I have signed my health proxy, arranged my funeral and ensured that I could remain at home. The only thing I haven't done is given any of my children my ATM passwords!

Two and a half years ago, my friend Peter Levine and his wife insisted on taking me to dinner the day I found out about my diagnosis. Peter had just given a guest sermon on challenges and hope, and he wanted to share his advice with me. I have since adapted my own version of it:

- Focus your energies on moving forward.
- Find a purpose that will help you do that by trying something new no matter how big or small, and focus on it. It's never too late to start.
- Take a chance. Accept the possibility that you might fail or not be good at what you are trying to do.
- Value your relationships with family and friends and maintain them. It's all right to accept support and help from them, just as you would be happy to offer it in return if necessary.
- Stop doing things you don't want to do. (I am still not very successful at this one.)
- Enjoy each and every day to the fullest.
- Above all, keep a sense of humor.

Ultimately, whatever our individual challenges, we all have to make decisions about how we want to live from day to day. In these past seven years, I have had some of the happiest moments of my life. Choosing how to live with cancer has given me an opportunity to make my own statement about survival.

EPILOGUE

One Small Star

Can your soul be out there somewhere
Beyond the infinity of time
I guess you've found some answers now
I'll have to wait for mine
Till my light joins with yours someday
To shine through time and space
And one day falls, in a distant age
Upon some stranger's face.

But your light still shines
It's one small star to guide me
And to help me hold back the dark
Your light's still shining in my heart.

Eric Bogle

So here I am. It is July 2009, and I have reached the final chapter of this book. I am facing my own final chapter, as well. The three tumors in my lungs, where the breast cancer metastasized, have begun to grow again a little, although my oncologist still considers my condition stable. I have been preoccupied with trying to figure out what all this means in terms of what will happen next, and when.

But this weekend, while I am digesting the import of my latest tests, I am driving to Gloucester, my favorite place in the entire world, to stay with my dear friends, Nancy and Michael Leavitt. We have been friends for over forty years. They have invited me to visit them every year since Bob died. We always drive past Good Harbor Beach, where Bob and I and the kids rented "Brown Boulder" all those years ago. The hundred-year-old homestead we all loved so much blew away in the No Name Storm several years ago, and the new home on the spot doesn't hold a candle to it. Nancy always makes dinner for long time friends, Herb Hurwitz and Judy Feldman and Mel and Martha Rosenblatt. We have lunch with my friend, Susie Cohan, who always reminds me that when she first moved to Worcester as a very young bride 54 years ago, I solicited her and explained why women needed to give separately from their husbands. We drive to "downtown" Gloucester, past the fishing fleets, and visit the charming little stores. I know this year will be just as familiar and special.

As I drive, I think back on how extraordinary the previous three months have been, especially in light of what is to come. One special thing after another has happened to me. In April, I came home a day early from Longboat Key to attend the White Coat Ceremony at UMass Medical School, where incoming third year medical students don white coats to mark their transition from preclinical studies to clinical health sciences. Typically, white coat ceremonies involve a formal "robing" or "cloaking" of students in white coats, the garb physicians have traditionally worn for over 100 years and that other health professionals have adopted.

Marcus Ruopp and J.P. Craford, who were in my geriatric clerkship two years ago, invited me to come. I was very touched. When I arrived in Mechanics Hall, I, too, was asked to wear a white coat because I was a faculty member! I really felt like an imposter as I marched with the faculty and sat on the stage. It was a very moving ceremony, and I must confess I enjoyed my "status" immensely.

A few weeks later, I reached the goal I had set for myself for the year: to be well enough to attend the Bat Mitzvah of my granddaughter, Becca. Because of my diagnosis, Becca had agreed to move the ceremony ahead by a year so that she became a Bat Mitzvah at the age of twelve instead of the usual thirteen. As a result, she had to learn two years of Hebrew in one. This didn't faze her a bit. She was spectacular: confident and self-assured. She went through the service like a pro. Except for two of my grandsons, my family was all there, including my sister, Jean, and brother, Joel, with his friend, Adrienne, and my dear in-law family, Alice Green and Elaine and Charlie Rosen. How lucky it has been for me that Bob's family was so loving and that we have always thought of each other as friends as well as family. Even Elaine and Charlie's children and grandchildren, with whom I am very close, were able to come. Rachel thought of everything, including scheduling the Bat Mitzvah for the day before Mother's Day, so we could all celebrate together again the next day.

The following week, the Mohegan Council of Boy Scouts honored me with their "Character Counts Award." I was surprised because I had never been involved with the Boy

Scouts, unless one counts my insistence on "always being prepared." It was a lovely ceremony. I now have a statue of a boy scout on my coffee table as a remembrance.

Three days later, I received an honorary degree from Clark University. As a trustee, I had attended over ten graduations and watched many others so honored. My dear friends, Denise Darrigrand, the Dean of Students at Clark, and Sharon Krefetz, a professor in the Government Department and head of the Urban Development program, had proposed my name. It was thrilling to be at the receiving end this year. There were wonderful festivities surrounding the event. I spoke to the students at Convocation in the morning and was hooded in the afternoon at Commencement. Sharon Krevitz read the citation, which meant a great deal to me. As the hood was placed over my head, I recall looking up and saying to myself, "You see, Mother, I did turn out all right. I do have value to many people." Once again, as over the years, my eyes filled up as I thought back to my childhood. But then I spied my daughters, Rachel and Patty, and Patty's husband, Rich, in the front row. I smiled and pushed away the thoughts that might have spoiled the occasion for me.

As if that weren't enough, I learned that the Women's Initiative was starting the Women's Initiative Fund in honor of Lois B. Green, which was intended "To Advance Women's Philanthropy for the Benefit of Women and Children." In addition, last December, my friend, Jenique LeBlond, started the Lois B. Green Health Policy Center on Aging at the Hebrew Senior Life's Institute for Aging Research. "My" Center will foster research on aging that results in health policies at the state and national levels to encourage dignity, respect and independence in the lives of older people.

I care deeply about both of these causes. What a lovely legacy to enjoy while I am alive!

A couple of days ago, I went to a party at the home of my friend, Patsy Lewis. Many of the women there had been my friends for years, quite a few as executive directors of agencies with whom I have worked. It was fun to hear them competing about how long they each had known me. I hired Dory O'Rourke to be the new executive at Edward Street Day Care Center about forty years ago. I hired Patsy at the United Way thirty years ago. And Linda Cavaioli, who was vice president in charge of fundraising at United Way when I became chairman, has known me for over twenty years. She refers to me as her "other" mother. Over the years, I have been so close to each of these women and so proud of them, as I have watched them grow in their careers, succeeding at one thing after another.

And yet, I am uncomfortable with the deference shown me. Inside, I am still the same Lois Green I was all those years ago. It's as though I have come full circle. I think back on how I admired my role models as a young woman, and I was always so awed by the attention they paid me. Isn't it strange that others may now view me in the same way. But as I draw closer to Gloucester, where the comfort of dear friends and the soothing sound of the sea await me, I am deeply aware of how lucky I am and have been. My troubled childhood might have left me with some emotional scars, yet I also learned to be strong and to value my close family. For almost fifty years, Bob and I were each other's best friends. I miss him every day. I adore my children, in-law children, and my grandchildren. Each and every day, when I open my eyes in the morning, I look up at the pictures on the walls surrounding me to see Sarah, David, Patty and Rachel as little children; pictures of Bob and me with the entire family; and the pictures I love of me with my nine grandchildren. I glance at each one and say good morning to Jesse, Gabe, Alex, Jeremy, Laura, Sammy, Andrea, Becca and Daniel and contemplate where they all are at this moment. Could anyone be happier or feel luckier than I? I don't think so.

I have also been so fortunate in the friends I have made, too many to name, as I have traveled from Drew Seminary to Bryn Mawr, Temple Emanuel to the United Way, Memorial Hospital to Clark University, the Jewish Federation to the Hoche-Schofield Foundation, from Worcester to Longboat Key. Each newly opened door has brought new experiences and challenges, wonderful friends and colleagues, and the opportunity to put my own talent, time and treasure to good use. I have loved every minute.

These thoughts drive away the more frightening ones. I have so much to look forward to: the one-mile Walk to Cure Cancer at UMass Medical School with my wonderful group of supporters, "Friends of Lois," helping to find a cure for this dreadful disease so that others will be able to live out their full lives; the Jewish holidays that have held so much meaning in my life, singing and chanting the prayers; the eighth year of my Geriatric Clerkship; another Thanksgiving in Longboat Key; and God willing, the celebration of my 80th birthday in August 2010, a goal that almost seems doable right now.

And so, as I reach Gloucester, I can say with great pride and satisfaction, Lois, you have written your last chapter, the one that really matters.

PHOTOS

Lois and her grandchildren

Bob's 76th birthday — 7/23/01

Thanksgiving 2008

The Siblings, circa 1978

My grandmother — Sarah P. Suisman

Breinigsville, PA USA
22 March 2010
234675BV00001B/1/P